PERFECT
in Memory

PERFECT
in Memory

A Son's Tribute to His Mother

Rick D. Niece, Ph.D.

FIVE STAR
PUBLICATIONS
Shining Brightly Since 1985

Chandler, Arizona

Linda F. Radke, President
Five Star Publications, Inc.
PO Box 6698
Chandler, AZ 85246-6698
480-940-8182
www.FiveStarPublications.com

www.rickniecebooks.com

Publisher's Cataloging-In-Publication Data

Names: Niece, Rick D.
Title: Perfect in memory : a son's tribute to his mother / Rick D. Niece, PhD.
Description: Chandler, Arizona : Five Star Publications,
    [2016] | Fanfare for a hometown series ; book 3
Identifiers: LCCN 2016931130 | ISBN 978-1-58985-238-9
    (paperback) | ISBN 978-1-58985-239-6 (ebook)
Subjects: LCSH: Niece, Dortha Jean Geyer. | Niece, Rick D.--Family. | Mothers--
    Biography. |DeGraff (Ohio)--Social life and customs--20th century.
Classification: lcc f496.4.n53 n54 2016 (print) | lcc
    f496.4.n53 (ebook) | DDC 977.1/043/092--dc23

Electronic edition provided by

The eDivision of Five Star Publications, Inc.

Printed in the United States of America

COVER & CHAPTER DESIGN: Kris Taft Miller
PAGE LAYOUT: Renana Typesetting
EDITOR: Paul M. Howey
PROOFREADERS: Ruthann Raitter and Cristy Bertini
PROJECT MANAGER: Patti Crane

This book is written with the intent of being as accurate as possible. It is based upon how the author remembers events and experiences.

Dedicated to . . .

Sherée ~ for Love

Dad ~ for Commitment

Jeff ~ for Humor

Kurt ~ for Creativity

Uncle Richard ~ for Devotion

Uncle Bob ~ for Advice

Hospice ~ for Compassion

DeGraff ~ for Memories

But most of all, to Mom ~ for Courage

Automythography

The books in the *Fanfare for a Hometown* series are auto-mythographies, a word I did not coin, but have redefined to apply to literature. An automythography is a work of nonfiction that looks reflectively at *what* we think we remember, and *how* we think we remember it. Automythographies are iridescent memories based upon the writer's truth and personal narrative. Soap bubbles, for example, are iridescent. They change color and shape as they float away, but they remain the same soap bubbles no matter how far they go. Memories do that as well. As they drift away from us, they alter in color and shape. They are, nonetheless, the same memories no matter how much time passes.

An autobiography is written by the author and spans the author's life chronologically. An automythography includes phases of the author's life in no particular order, while focusing on specific memories and the people who helped make those memories.

The stories in an automythography are not made up. They are based on true events. They become "myth" by being passed down and repeated, written, and remembered. That is the nature of memory, and it is the essence of an automythography.

RDN

An Introduction
MAHLER

Mom feared death. Throughout her life she was neither overly nor underly religious. She was simply religious, and I have always considered that to be an enviable compromise. Even so, she feared death.

When my mother was seventy-two, a doctor told my father that his wife had perhaps five years to live, because a disease with no cure was invading her lungs. This insidious disease would eventually deny her oxygen, he told Dad, leaving her literally in a death stranglehold. The doctor told this to our father, who told his sons, who were made to promise not to tell their mother. It's possible she knew anyway, but she never discussed it. Nor, for that matter, did she talk with us about any of the other things she feared.

Mom lived three years beyond the doctor's five-year prognosis. I believe that death was as wary of her as she was of it, and therefore was hesitant to move in too quickly. Death can be strangely courteous sometimes and cautiously slow to act. Besides, mothers have a way of keeping the upper hand on most things dreadful.

My parents moved to Arizona from Ohio after Dad's retirement as a music teacher. They sought a climate warmer and friendlier to their health. The other reason they chose Tucson was because my younger brothers lived there. Jeff had his own construction company, and Kurt owned an art gallery. Two decades later, during the final years of Mom's life, they also rented the guesthouse located next to the president's home on the campus of the University of the Ozarks in Clarksville, Arkansas. They established a routine in which they would remain in Arkansas from May until October, then scurry back to Tucson to avoid any chance of experiencing winter's triplets of cold, snow, and ice. Having lived through Ohio's wintery months for all of their working years, they'd had enough of layered clothing.

Mom's final months in Arkansas were difficult for her—and for us. Her ability to breathe continued to diminish, and with it, her zest for life. She gradually began to lose interest in the activities she'd always enjoyed: conversation, reading, and a decades-old tradition of three-handed pinochle with Dad and me. She became less aware and more withdrawn, preferring to sit quietly in the Queen Anne chair she'd salvaged from Uncle Ude's farmhouse. She'd had it refurbished by one of my old DeGraff newspaper route customers. As she sat, she often struggled through rattling starts and stops for even the shallowest snatches of life-giving air.

A promise I had made to Sherée to write about my childhood in DeGraff gained new urgency. I decided to write the stories to appease my wife and to please my mother. The plan was to read them to Mom as she rested in Queen Anne's comfort while receiving supplemental oxygen through a cannula in her nose. Through my stories, I secretly hoped she might breathe in streams of rejuvenating oxygen from the lungs of life's good memories relived.

I wrote whenever I could find the time. And when I did, the writing was intense, occurring early in the morning, late at night, in airports, during flights, and on frequent road trips to visit university donors, alumni, and friends. Days and nights were filled with hours of writing and revising, revising and writing. I wanted my stories to be as perfect as possible before I read them to her.

During the late afternoon walk back from my campus office to our university home, I'd stop to visit with Mom and Dad. It was obvious she enjoyed the time we spent together, however brief, and eagerly listened to every word about my often uneventful day as university president.

For me, these visits had a second purpose. I was using my mother as a "Rickie's boyhood in DeGraff" fact-checker. I wanted the details of my remembrances to be as accurate as possible. She possessed an encyclopedic warehouse of memory-rich information, and even in declining health, her knack for retaining precise minutiae of seemingly insignificant triviality never ceased to astound me. Mom was an oral memorialist, a keeper of exactness, and an unpaid "graduate research assistant" I could count on for correctness. During our moments of reflection, she seemed to regain some of the dignity the disease had stolen from her, and I think we both breathed more easily.

When I was an infant—the time before any real memory keeping began—my father was a piano major at the Oberlin College Conservatory of Music in Oberlin, Ohio. During his recitals and the conservatory's orchestral and choral concerts, Mom told me she would cradle me close to her breast and hum the performance melodies into my welcoming ears. I believe this early exposure to classical music, both subliminal and significant, gifted me with a lifetime of appreciation for the masters.

As the disease continued to tighten its grip on my mother, I hoped her love for classical music might provide some relief, even if only slight. Between the moments of her validating my DeGraff childhood memories, I'd remind her about our most admired composer, Gustav Mahler. I especially wanted her to remember our shared Mahler favorite: his second symphony, the "Resurrection." Try as I might, I am unable to connect with Mahler in the same exceptional manner she did.

Mahler also feared death, and that might have been one of the reasons my mother revered him so much. He began writing the "Resurrection" after a frightening vision in which he had seen himself laid out upon a funeral bier surrounded by flowers, while an ominous organ dirge droned on. Writing this titanic symphony, which contains five movements instead of the standard four, consumed six years of Mahler's life. Within that span of time, he created a colossal opus, binding life and afterlife—from birth to death to resurrection.

During the extraordinary final movement, after an extended thunderstorm of instrumental blends, a celestial chorus of pastoral voices rises from the rumbling like a silken mist. No written description can adequately express the impassioned serenity the music lays upon the listener. For that reason, the fifth movement would render my mother speechless each time she heard it (a miraculous achievement in and of itself). Because of this vivid memory I have of her, the music still reduces me to tears.

The chorus sings in German whispers, "Rise again, yes thou shall rise again." Measures later, a singular voice, alone and outside the chorus, murmurs back in a far off, yet oh so close assurance, "You were not born in vain." The musical dialogue between the chorus and this angelic voice subdues all earthly debate. With orchestral and choral confidence, the symphonic

4

journey of life, death, and afterlife soars to climactic conclusion, and then closes its eyes.

To hearten Mom as she sat in her Queen Anne chair and to remind her of kinder times, I looked forward to reading my manuscript to her, with Mahler playing inconspicuously conspicuous in the background. I wanted us to share my remembrances about life in DeGraff, our family, and Bernie Jones. Although the stories were promised for Sherée, this gift was to be for my mother.

I was still writing when my parents left in October for Arizona. I was confident they would return to Arkansas in May. Dad returned, but Mom did not. There were no readings and no music.

I should have started sooner.

A Concept of Heaven

I cannot help but think
that when I die
no one,
except an awaiting angel,
will notice.

An angel
dressed in white-pink and wrinkles
and looking so much
like a someone's mother.
An angel
with crinkled wings and sadappy eyes
who watched over a son's lifetime
of trying.

And when I drift to my infinity,
there will be a communion—
simple
silent
pre-prenatal.

Then
cradled,
I will rest.

PART I

Chapter One
PAULA WILLS

Paula Wills knows not to interrupt me when I am greeting prospective students. When they and their parents tour campuses in their search for just the right fit, I believe university presidents owe them a few minutes of uninterrupted conversation. Their potential long-term commitment is far greater than any alteration in a president's otherwise rigid schedule. Personally, I enjoy these impromptu visits to my office. You can understand then why I was a little perturbed when Paula slipped into my office to announce I had a telephone call.

Immediately prior to that, the young lady's mother was in the middle of what sounded to me to be a finely rehearsed monologue in which she was detailing her cheerleader, dance team captain, prom queen, honor roll daughter's "aspiration since she was four years old" to be a pediatric cardiologist. The husband/father/silent partner in tow just smiled as he nodded with metronome-like regularity throughout his wife's spiel. As always, I attempted a look of reinforcing admiration while crafting a clever and hopefully sincere-sounding response. University presidents must appear to be genuine even within periodic bouts of disingenuousness. That's what I was doing when Paula interrupted.

Paula is a campus legend at the University of the Ozarks. With her perfect credentials, she had served as the executive assistant to presidents for years before my arrival and avowed to serve in the same capacity for me until her well-planned retirement seven years hence. As the wrong side of the Mason-Dixon Line, newly-hired damn Yankee on campus and in town, I knew full well I needed a person of her status, experience, and reputation to cover what was certain to be my very vulnerable backside. I was also warned that novice presidents who did not gain her trust failed to become veteran presidents.

In an indirect manner, Paula was responsible for my securing a long-term commitment from the board of trustees. She informed the board chair, Dallas big-time lawyer Ed Smith, that she was not about to break in any more rookies. I was to be her last presidential project before retirement. Since no one, not even an esteemed Texas attorney, dared argue a case against Paula Wills, I picked up my favorite Parker fountain pen and signed a multi-year contract. Paula and Ed sealed the deal with approving nods and self-satisfied winks. Fortified with guaranteed employment and Paula safeguarding my career, I was almost as secure as a tenured professor.

This wasn't the first time Paula had interrupted one of my meetings with a prospective student. During my initial month as president, she had come into my office frantically waving the telephone like Leonard Bernstein conducting the New York Philharmonic. She insisted this was a call I needed to take *immediately*. I attempted to motion her away with a slight wave of the hand, but Paula did not budge. I waved a second, more emphatic gesture, and again no movement. I then calmly suggested she take a message for me. She frowned, took a giant step forward, and jabbed the phone at me like an Olympic fencer. I took a baby step backward while repeating my take-a-message order. As we parried, she armed with a telephone and I weaponless, the young man and his parents with whom I had been meeting watched in wide-eyed astonishment. Paula finally conceded. While leaving my office, she mouthed in silent smugness, "You will be sorry." I had no idea why I'd be sorry, but I feared she was no doubt correct.

I finished with the visiting family and waited until Paula left for lunch before retrieving the pink message slip strategically placed atop my inbox on her desk. She had triple checked the "urgent" listing on the slip's priority choices. I slumped when I read who had called. It had been Mrs. Helen Walton.

Helen Walton was the widow of Wal-Mart founder Sam Walton, and she served as the honorary lifetime chair of the University of the Ozarks' Board of Trustees. Below Mrs. Walton's name, Paula had written in her flawlessly cursive script, "See, I told you to take this call!" Her admonition worked, and I felt duly chastised. Weak-kneed, I wobbled into my office, certain the kettledrum pounding in my chest was a percussion overture to a suddenly shortened lifespan.

Mrs. Walton is a lady of well-deserved admiration, and she had conducted the fifth and final presidential interview with Sherée and me. She *really* liked Sherée, and as a happy consequence, I was offered the presidency at Ozarks. To no one's surprise, especially not Mrs. Walton's, Sherée soon became the best collegiate first lady in the universe.

With shaking hands and panic pinching my throat, I dialed Mrs. Walton's private number. On the second ring she answered, "This is Helen." I identified myself, and she thanked me for returning her call.

I apologized for not talking to her earlier and explained that I was meeting with a prospective student and his parents. She laughed and confided that Sam often did not take her calls either, no matter how urgent they were, especially if he was meeting with potential suppliers or customers. She agreed with my choice to remain with the campus visitors, and assured me Sam would have done the same thing. Her words put me at ease. We discussed enrollment and the need for a new residence hall, her purpose for the call.

Paula must have fretted about our incident during lunch. She apologized when she returned, and after I told her about my conversation with Mrs. Walton, she repeated that she was genuinely sorry to have caused a fuss. From that day on, God bless her, Paula never again interrupted me while I was meeting with prospective students and their parents—until now.

When she stepped hesitantly into my office, Paula had the phone cradled against her hip. "I am sorry to intrude," she whispered, "but this is your brother Kurt calling from Arizona. He sounds upset. I think you should speak with him." I didn't argue. She handed me the telephone, and I excused myself. I had a bad feeling as I walked into the conference room next to my office and closed the door.

"Kurt, what's going on?"

"It's Mom. She's in the hospital and has taken a turn for the worse. Even though they have increased her oxygen, it doesn't seem to be enough. You and Sherée need to get to Tucson as soon as possible. Dad is not handling any of this well. Jeff and I are afraid she doesn't have much time. You need to come now."

I promised Kurt we would be there the next day. I knew my mother feared death, and now I feared it for her.

I stood for the longest time without moving. I was aware I wasn't moving. I was aware of the winter scene framed by the conference room windows. I was aware of the barren trees and lifeless grass. And I was aware I was quietly crying. Beyond that, I was aware of little else.

I hugged Paula and told her why Sherée and I needed to go to Tucson. Forgetting my winter coat, I hurried home. For some reason I stopped in front of the now vacant Ozarks' guesthouse. Through the front window, I could see Mom's Queen Anne chair in the living room's shadows. Spits of rain turning into sleet turning into snow turned into visions of my family and our life in DeGraff. I froze, and the memories swirled around me, gathering themselves to give me comfort.

Chapter Two
MOM

My mother's name was Dortha Jean, but everyone knew her as Dode or Dodie. Her maiden name was Geyer, and she came from strong German ancestry. We spent more holidays with her side of the family than with Dad's, in what I can only presume was an agreeable arrangement between them. Mom is the eldest of three children, and consequently, I am the eldest among my maternal cousins.

My mother's life was forever marked by two intertwined, tragic incidents. Her mother, Naomi, died from leukemia when she was just thirty-seven years old. And then Mom's father, Grandpa Jack, disappeared after his wife's funeral. He left without an explanation or forwarding address. Mom, only sixteen at the time, was suddenly the caretaker of her two younger brothers—thirteen-year-old Richard and three-year-old Bob. Bob's full name was Robert Dean, and in tribute to my uncles, my parents named me Richard Dean.

Just two months after the funeral, the electric and gas were shut off for non-payment. Their Uncle John came to the rescue by paying utility bills and buying groceries, but the three were still very much on their own. In time, the responsibility became too much for Mom, and Grandma Houchin, the family stalwart of legendary status, removed them from their lives in Huntington, Indiana, and brought them to live with her on the family farm in Lakeview, Ohio.

Ulys, nicknamed Ude, was Mom's maternal uncle. He also lived on the farm with Grandma Houchin, his mother. The dramatic move to Lakeview was particularly difficult for Mom who, as a senior in high school, was forced to leave her hometown and classmates.

Grandpa Jack eventually returned, but he wasn't alone. He brought with him a new wife and her young daughter from another marriage. According to family gossip (and I stress this is gossip with no verifiable proof), she was a woman of suspicious reputation he met in Indianapolis. Although their marriage didn't last, the resentment it created did, and my mother spent much of her life acting as a mediator during the years-long, back-and-forth acrimony between her father and her brothers.

During the span of Grandpa Jack's second marriage and the resultant family turmoil, Bob, the youngest, was passed among various caregivers. He was taken from Grandma Houchin's and sent to Toledo to live with his Uncle Glen and Aunt Uarda. After a brief time with them, his father and stepmother decided they wanted him, and so he was returned to Lima. Unfortunately, that arrangement quickly disintegrated, and they placed young Bob in a Marsh Foundation facility, a home for unwanted children. Not long after that, Grandpa Jack and his second wife divorced. A few years later, Grandpa Jack found renewed marital happiness with his third wife, Ruth, the grandmother I came to know and love.

Although the Marsh Foundation environment was a stable one for Bob, the thought of him not being with family finally became unbearable for Mom, and my parents brought him home to live with us in DeGraff. My mother and her brother were together again. He was now fifteen, and at age five I had a big-brother-like uncle.

Not until he graduated from high school and joined the navy did I realize the impact my uncle's embittered childhood had on him. Little kids are often oblivious to the heartaches around them. Bob's early transient homelife coupled with his inexplicable abandonment resulted in permanent resentment. He could not forgive his father. Because I loved both my Uncle Bob and my Grandpa Jack, I tried to understand both sides but never could.

We spent every Fourth of July with Mom's family, and the celebrations inevitably turned into multiday marathons. Our house became the annual holiday resort because we had a swimming pool, lawn croquet, a horseshoe pit, a front yard for football, Wiffle ball, and badminton, and a basketball court in the old barn on our edge-of-town property. Eventually, we even cemented the driveway for singles and doubles tennis matches. We'd play games during the day and cards late into the night, and for every event, indoor and outdoor, the competition was intense.

To this day, I am embarrassed by what a poor loser and arrogant winner I was. I'm pretty sure I came by it naturally. Dad never lost a badminton match during our many Fourth of July gatherings. He was the undisputed, undefeated, unflappable, and equally unbearable grand champion.

One summer, Cousin Mike declared he had practiced badminton all year with a semiprofessional player and was ready to dethrone the champion. Dad, however, did not panic. His game was built on strong defense, and that meant he seldom had to exert much energy to win. All of us surrounded the court, and in less-than-dignified Wimbledon fashion, we rooted for Mike. The cheers against my father were in vain. In short order, the match ended in victory for Dad with poor Cousin Mike lying spent on the ground.

Humiliated and still flat on his back, Mike served the royalist of all swear words straight toward Dad, and all ears big and small heard it. It turned out to be Mike's only successful serve of the day, and he aced it! I can still see the startled look on Mom's face, Aunt Sally's death stare, Uncle Richard's despair, and Dad's impish grin. Those of us gathered to watch knew his curse was the vilest of all forbidden words, but we giggled in delight nonetheless.

All of us enjoyed the Fourth of July in DeGraff, especially Uncle Richard, Aunt Sally, and their four children. My cousins—Pam, Mike, Debbie, and Betsy—looked forward to a favorite adventure with my brothers and me: exploring dilapidated, abandoned houses around town and out in the country. We convinced one another each house was haunted, and to validate our belief, we'd cautiously visit them at twilight. Creaks, moans, thuds, rattles, and eerie sounds shadowed us from room to musty room. We could barely wait to scream, squeal, and scamper from the haunted premises to sprawl safely on the ground a good distance away. We'd then huddle close together for protection and to replay what we had seen, heard, and felt. The real purpose, however, was to scare ourselves all over again. These many decades later, we continue to retell our ghost stories and swear they are true. In a way, I wish they were.

Pam was my favorite cousin, and we were close in age and thick in secrets. Whenever we needed another football player, I tried my best to convince her to be one of the guys. Once, she agreed to join us, but only once. I can still see her wearing a helmet and going deep for one of my passes, but the meandering route she took entangled her in Mom's favorite rose trellis. No one was happy about the outcome—not Pam, not Mom, not Aunt Sally, and certainly not me. I was especially unhappy because, as I remember it, Pam was wide open before she decided to improvise the play and slant left instead of right. She still cannot explain why.

Each morning began with two greatly anticipated rituals: preparation of the homemade ice cream and the mixing of a potent pitcher of lime vodka. The lime vodka, an alcoholic drink concocted by Dad and Aunt Sally, was off-limits to any of us kids, and for the most part we obeyed. A notable exception occurred one extremely hot afternoon when Jeff and Mike mysteriously got into the forbidden green inebriant, later claiming they thought they were consuming limeade. Both slept soundly through that evening's fireworks display. Fingers were pointed at Uncle Bob for having something to do with the escapade, but he never owned up to it.

Mom was in charge of cooking the pudding-like custard for our indescribably delicious homemade ice cream, and like a clandestine laboratory chemist, she kept the ingredients secret. She'd arise early in the morning to gather, measure, mix, and cook the sweet smelling, thickly textured, elixir-like richness of golden-colored goodness. Any time one of us ventured too close to the stove, she'd spread her arms wide to conceal the bubbling pot like one of Macbeth's witches hovering over the boiling cauldron. Thankfully, in my mother's case, the eye of newt, toe of frog, and leg of lizard were not among the unspoken ingredients.

Mom controlled the amount of ice cream scooped out for each one of us. She was a consistent single dipper, no matter how much we complained about our measured rations. Although outwardly miffed by the limited portions, I knew deep down there was only so much for so many. She was not a loaves-and-fish miracle worker. Looking back on it, I understand the broader lesson she was teaching: a little bit of something good keeps us appreciative, while too much spoils us.

During one memorable Fourth of July celebration, and after at least two glasses too many of the infamous lime vodka, Mom coyly declared she was going to reveal the ice cream recipe. Our jabbering crew quieted to pin-drop silence. After tapping an empty glass with her ring, she slurrily told us that the recipe was Grandma Houchin's, the one fact we already knew. We tottered on the edge of our seats pleading for more, and she began to deliver. She continued by announcing she had discovered her own method for making the custard even richer, creamier, and smoother than Grandma Houchin's recipe. She boasted that she made hers better by tripling two of the ingredients and adding...

That was the end of her proclamation. Before uttering another syllable, she slipped softly onto the couch, curled up, and fell asleep. Mike again mumbled the forbidden word, the same word I'll bet the rest of us were thinking. Disappointed, we moaned in unison before herding en masse to the kitchen for more ice cream. With the little dipper down for the count, big dipper Bob scooped out more generous helpings.

There was no secret recipe for cranking the old-fashioned ice cream maker that magically transformed Mom's custard into frozen deliciousness. The work was hard, especially the last hundred cranks, and as we neared the end, we'd count down the final ten in unison. Regardless of age, we were all required to take a churning turn, but the adults were the only ones permitted to sprinkle rock salt on the crushed ice inside the wooden bucket. The salt quickened the melting of the ice as we, with aching arms, whirled the recipe into obscenely rich mounds of butter-yellow delight. If any salt escaped through the cap of the rotating custard-containing cylinder, the mixture would be ruined, and my mother's wrath would rain down upon us.

Throughout our many Fourth of July ice cream celebrations, I recall only one batch being ruined, and my Uncle Richard bravely accepted the blame. That day we sadly spooned DeGraff Creamery ice cream, famous throughout Ohio for its high standard but vastly inferior compared to Mom's.

Over the years our holiday tradition slowly died among a wave of marriages, geographic relocations, additional commitments, and understandable new traditions. Mom eventually shared the treasured recipe for homemade ice cream with Pam. Growing older, sicker, and weaker, she didn't want the recipe to go to the grave with her. Pam, the family loyalist, waited out her self-imposed statute of limitations before divulging the secret to her sister Debbie. Even now, each understands her anointed role of privilege, and the ingredients remain safely cloaked in mystery.

I hold precious the memory of my mother preparing the family's Fourth of July delicacy. I'd give almost anything for all of us to gather together one last time. And I would savor the feast of a single dip.

I gained an appreciation from my mother for the pleasure of reading and respect for the written word. She also taught me the art of listening and relating to others on a personal level. Mom never met a stranger, and her ability to carry on a conversation with anyone, anywhere, at any time amazed me. People waiting in line with her would hear more than they needed to know about her three boys, and would be questioned about their own families. You could learn a lot about life—your own and someone else's—while standing in line with my mother.

Mom stayed home to raise her sons. She was a housewife and proud of it. Domestication was her job, a position she believed she was born for. Oh, she did have occasional doubts about her life's choice, usually after a daytime talk show host tried to make her feel guilty about not having a "real" career. When my brothers and I assured her we valued her decision, she stopped believing in television's talking heads. Having lost her mother at such an early age, she appreciated our appreciation of having a mother around to raise us. And we did.

I Never Saw My Mother Cry

I never saw my mother cry
And do not know the reason why.
My father yes, but mother no.
Sometimes I wish it were not so.

The pain she kept was deep and raw—
An early death, her father's flaw.
Soft, healing tears I never saw.
I question now, then pause in awe.

How could she build that stoic wall
While sacrificing for us all?
A masking face concealing pall
Did not allow her tears to fall.

But who am I to question why
I never saw my mother cry?

Chapter Three
DAD

My father remains a major influence on my life and career. So much so that he deserves his own book.

Dad is the youngest of four children and the first in his family to graduate from college. His two brothers and sister were highly successful in the business world, and as a teacher, Dad was the less wealthy but highly respected family anomaly.

His oldest brother Garry founded and managed a manufacturing plant in South Lyons, Michigan. Even beyond his retirement, he held a variety of income-producing patents. Brother Melvin worked for Cadillac in Detroit, and later supervised design engineers for the school bus manufacturer, Superior Coach. Although he did not have a four-year degree, he earned the respect of the highly educated engineers he supervised. My uncles were true self-made men.

Sister LaVelva and her husband Robert owned and operated two grain elevators. Every farmer in their part of Ohio traveled to them with their grain because they paid the best price. Plus,

Uncle Robert was a world-class whistler, and his birdcalls were perfect imitations. Farmers from miles around pulled their filled wagons to his elevators, not only to be paid fairly, but to hear his avicular calls. I was so impressed by him and his talent that for years I wanted to be a professional whistler.

My Aunt LaVelva remains the classiest, most beautiful, and most refined lady I have ever known. She walked, talked, and dressed with elegance. She was even able to eat watermelon and corn on the cob in no-mess style. I never saw her wear the same outfit twice (a phenomenon that seemed to annoy my mother), and her taste in clothing was impeccable.

Aunt LaVelva had a copy of all of my publications displayed on their living room bookcase, and she always had a question or compliment about my latest publication, usually the poetry. She loved poetry, and I enjoyed reading her my latest poems. I never wanted to disappoint her.

Dad's family members possessed an amazing work ethic, made excellent livings, and were political conservatives with distrust for labor unions. My mother's family, on the other hand, was well populated with liberal Democrats and union members. As a youngster, I was fascinated by the heated debates and rapid-fire flare-ups that volleyed back and forth between my mother and any opponent from Dad's family who took a stand against her liberal ideology. Her primary opposition was Uncle Melvin, and the two of them had some battles that were doozies. Sitting ringside, Dad seldom offered his opinion. I was molded by those early encounters, and as a result, I am a hybrid of both families. I profess a middle of the road moderation and am able to see the bountiful good and bad of both major parties. Neutrality has its purpose.

Because Dad is the youngest in his family, my brothers and I are the youngest among the paternal set of cousins. At Niece family gatherings, I tried to shed my little brothers and join the big cousins. My attempts at integration were seldom successful, however, and looking back on it, I was undoubtedly a miniature irritation.

I have vivid memories of one particular Easter. We had gone to my grandparents' house to celebrate, and I couldn't wait to show my older cousins the Avon soap pistol the Easter Bunny had gifted me. But my excitement was short-lived, and I was taught two painful lessons.

First, after Cousins Ron, Don, and Dennis snatched the soap pistol away from me and gleefully rubbed it under an outside water spigot, I learned that Avon soap pistols melt quickly into bubbled oblivion. They were proud of their fragrantly clean hands. My other cousins, including sweet Penny, thought their cleansing deed was funny and clever. I felt as squished as the pistol.

Second, I learned the Easter Bunny is not real. Larry and David, the oldest male cousins and my idols, broke the shattering news to me. I had gone to my grandparents' house soap-gun armed and Easter happy, but left weaponless and disillusioned. I guess I should have been able to figure out, even in my pint-sized gullibility, that the Easter Bunny would not have access to the Avon lady. My only good fortune was having enough sense to leave the solid chocolate bunny at home. Since I now knew it was not a direct descendent of the Easter Bunny, I gnawed its ears off without a tinge of guilt.

Dad was my music teacher in all twelve years of school, first grade through graduation. I was proud to call him "Dad" in and out of the classroom. He taught every music-related offering in the curriculum, including the concert and marching bands, chorus, and music appreciation classes.

Our high school had 150 students during my senior year. In a remarkable tribute to his musical influence, one hundred of them sang in chorus and eighty played in one or more of the bands. Confident in his abilities, Dad claimed he could teach anyone to sing, even off-key-couldn't-carry-a-tune-in-a-laundry-basket "atonals" like John Slater and Mike Melhorn. They were as tone-deaf as Donald Duck and true chorus clinkers, but Dad never gave up on them. Participation, not perfection, was his goal.

He is the real-life music man to so many of us. But best of all, he is my dad.

Chapter Four
JEFF

Brother Jeff, the middle son, is the comic in our family. No one makes me laugh like he can. His stories, sworn to be true, are clever mixtures of truth, fiction, and pure whimsy. Through the years, his tales have affectionately become known as "Jeffisms."

His first "public performance" occurred in church when he was four. During the Children's Message, delivered as we crowded together on the floor at the front of the sanctuary, the minister gave each of us a Jesus bookmarker. Jeff excitedly clutched the gift in his tiny fist, jumped up, and shouted, "Holy crap, Mom, look what I got!"

The minister tried to stare Jeff down, but he eventually gave up. He stopped his remarks in mid-parable, turning to the congregation and asking them to pray for Jeff. Basking in this sudden recognition—and never one to miss the spotlight—Jeff turned and bowed to his audience. Even today, he claims "holy crap" is a religious proclamation reverently chanted among an ostracized order of Himalayan monks.

Jeff's disadvantage was being the middle child. He was too young to hang out with me and too old for Kurt and his friends. Thus is the truth about the middle child syndrome, and Jeff has lived a lifetime of it. In our school system, no teacher ever moved on, retired, or died before teaching at least two generations of the same family. I think it was written into their annual contracts and caused tenure to be revered in DeGraff. Even though Jeff was smarter than I and was a better athlete, teachers and coaches too often failed to notice it. Instead, they consistently referred to him as Rickie Niece's little brother.

Jeff and I were decent athletes. I played second base and batted leadoff in Little League, Pony League, and high school. And so did Jeff. I played point guard on the junior high and high school basketball teams. And so did Jeff. In track, as did I, Jeff ran the 100-yard dash, the 220, the 880 relay, and the low hurdles. But here the similarities trail off. Jeff was a star quarterback in high school and a champion wrestler. I was not. It wasn't until our family moved from DeGraff to Kent for Dad's new position at Kent State University that Jeff emerged from my shadow and cast an even bigger one for himself.

Jeff did truly eclipse me in one area. Compared to me, he was by far the ornerier. For example, he never met a parent-imposed curfew he agreed with. On numerous occasions, Dad would greet Jeff at the back door as he valiantly attempted to sneak into the house after hours. Although a cagy one, Jeff could not out-cage our father, and he was grounded more times than airplanes at O'Hare in January. Being out of commission, however, never seemed to deter him or his legion of girlfriends-in-waiting. Jeff relished his James Dean image in opposition to my Opie Taylor one, and the contrast succeeded in setting us apart.

A rebel with a cause, Jeff never liked being told what to do. A perfect example of his defiance occurred one Christmas when he was nine years old and received the gift of a BB gun. Although it was not the famous Red Ryder model, the gun was a dandy. Before allowing Jeff to venture outside and test his new weapon, Dad made a plainly clear request. "Do not go down to the pasture and shoot at Ernie's cows." Ernie and Jinny Knief were our next-door neighbors on the outskirts of town where they planted crops and maintained a small herd of cattle. Because Ernie loved his cows and the fresh butter Jinny churned from their sweet milk, Dad's plea was a valid one.

Fancying himself as DeGraff's Lucas "The Rifleman" McCain, the protector of townfolk, Jeff disappeared quickly. Within minutes of his departure, our doorbell rang. It was Ernie. After an abrupt Christmas greeting and gift of molasses cookies from Jinny, Ernie got straight to the point. "Lewie and Dode, at this very moment Jeff is crouched down behind the creek bank in the pasture, and he is shooting at my cows. He thinks no one can see him. Let me guess. By some amazing coincidence did you give him a BB gun for Christmas?"

Dad paled while stammering a barely audible, "Yes, we did." Mom, as I have mentioned, was seldom ever at a loss for words. On this occasion, she was speechless.

"Wonderful choice," Ernie admonished. He just stood there shaking his head with his ever-present pipe gripped tightly between his clenched teeth. It pained me to watch this living naïveté scene starring frankly incensed wise man Ernie and my not-so-golden, mirthless parents.

After several seconds of Christmas cheerlessness, Ernie said, "Do you want to disarm Jeff or shall I?" Dad granted Ernie the privilege. As Ernie grumbled out the door, he fired back his own shot. "And one more thing. This time I will be the adult who grounds Jeff. I want it to stick. You two have any problem with that?" He didn't wait for an answer.

Jeff was grounded for two weeks, a house record, and while he served his sentence, I enjoyed using his gun to mow down tin cans. I was almost as ecstatic as Ernie and his cattle. As far as I know, Jeff never shot at another cow. But after that Christmas, the once-menacing bulldog belonging to another neighbor cowered whenever Jeff approached.

Jeff still maintains that he wasn't shooting at Ernie's cows. He claims they simply, one by one, wandered into his sights. Then he grins.

Although no one in our family is very tall, at five feet four inches, Jeff is the shortest. To his credit, I don't think he ever thought of himself as being short. That changed during a Niece family reunion when he was in his early twenties. It was on that day Jeff came face-to-face with his stature.

We had a relative who hadn't been back to Ohio for years, but he finally returned for this reunion at our grandparents' house. Jeff and I had never met him. His given name was Theodore, but to the family he was known as Uncle Shorty, an appropriate nickname for obvious reasons. He was a diminutive man. During the requisite family photo, Uncle Melvin placed Jeff in the front row next to Shorty. As the two of them eyeballed one another, Jeff anguished in the inescapable realization that he was an inch shorter than Shorty!

Jeff quickly disappeared after the picture-taking session. When I finally found him sneaking a smoke behind the garage, he didn't look up as I approached, but the despair in his voice said it all. "Holy crap, I'm shorter than Uncle Shorty. I can't believe it. I'm shorter than Shorty!" I did my brotherly best, of course, to reinforce that, yes, indeed he was.

Uncle Shorty appears quite pleased in that reunion picture. Jeff, on the other hand, looks beyond forlorn. For a variety of reasons, Jeff never returned for another Niece reunion. During each subsequent gathering I attended, Uncle Shorty always made me promise to say hello to my little brother Jeff for him. It's been many years since Shorty's passing, but I still enjoy telephoning Jeff and greeting him with, "Uncle Shorty says hey."

A Tribute in Haiku and Senryu to My Childhood Pasture

Deer fly
stalking the hunter
stalking the prey.

Cottonwoods lightly
salt the waving green acres.
Blackbirds walk across.

Frost arrived last night
and left winter's signature
etched on bended blades.

Udders stiff leg it
to the barn and stroking hands.
Milkweed drips behind.

Stepping-stones polished
sleekly in the pasture's creek—
wet without warning.

Chapter Five
KURT

Kurt is the youngest of our clan. At family get-togethers, birth order again kicks in, and much to his chagrin, he is little Kurtie again. I don't help the situation. He will always be my baby brother.

He had a rough beginning. With two sons already, my parents had hoped for a daughter. Because of the way Mom carried Kurt during her pregnancy, they were convinced he'd be a girl. After his birth and her disappointing discovery, Mom refused to hold him for the first hour. Rejection is difficult at any age. When she finally agreed to take him, his roughed up little face from the difficult delivery put her off for another hour. Motherly love, of course, eventually triumphed.

As a result of their daughter certainty, my parents hadn't considered boys' names. Since their baby looked like a professional boxer had pounded him, Dad wanted to name him Rock after Rocky Marciano, the only heavyweight champion to retire undefeated. Mom was appalled and quickly counterpunched.

Kirk Douglas was her favorite actor, and in his honor she chose Kirk. Jealous of his wife's infatuation with another man, Dad refused. They finally compromised on Kurt R., the initial "R" being as close as Dad could come to Rock.

I loved him immediately, and happily assumed the role of being my little brother's keeper. Jeff never required a keeper. As a child, Kurt was artistic, sensitive, and recondite. I somehow knew in time I'd learn more from him than he would from me. My worst mistake was trying to force him into athletics, and I still feel guilty about the agony I put him through. Athletics were important during my adolescent years, and I assumed he'd be drawn to sports, too. I was wrong, and it took me far too long to realize that drawing, designing, and decorating were more important to him than any athletes. He admired Rodin more than Ruth, Gauguin more than Groza, and Chagall more than Chamberlain.

I should have recognized his talents sooner. At age five, he redecorated his bedroom and eventually every room in the house. His gifted hands and creative eyes beautified lampshades, table-tops, China cabinets, kitchen utensil drawers, closets, bookcases, furniture, and even our musty basement.

Although we lived on the outskirts of DeGraff, we were nonagrarians who didn't utilize the property's barn, chicken coop, and equipment shed for their intended purposes. Instead, we converted the barn into a basketball court and used the shed and chicken coop for storage.

One summer, Dad decided we needed to cement our gravel driveway. He reasoned that the hard surface could double as a tennis court and allow him to humble even more relatives during the Fourth of July gatherings. The project took most of the summer and tons of concrete. Dad purchased a second-hand cement mixer, and under the expert supervision of Uncles Richard and Bob (Dad was famously known around DeGraff as Three-Tool Lewie, the unhandiest man in town), we built a tennis court that rivaled the ones you'd find at the US Open, at least by humble DeGraff standards.

Kurt and his best friend, Mike Elliot, also sought a summer project, so they decided to convert the equipment shed into a clubhouse. With Dad's blessing, they emptied the shed's contents into the chicken coop. While we toiled to complete the grand tennis court complex, Kurt and Mike transformed the shed into an exquisite clubhouse the Little Rascals would have admired. They furnished their dwelling with chairs, end tables, throw rugs, lamps, a bookcase, and an old radio. They then decorated the walls with posters and pictures. The place had everything. Well, it had just about everything. What it didn't have was a cement mixer.

Once we completed the tennis court surface, Dad, ever the pragmatist, moved his cement mixer into the shed. His decision was final no matter how much Kurt and Mike pouted as we rolled the massive mixer into their space. The obstacle created a new challenge for this preteen duo of decorators, but they were up to the challenge.

After Kurt and Mike had quietly retreated to their clubhouse for a couple of hours, I became curious and decided to investigate. When I entered, I discovered two self-satisfied smilers seated at what appeared to be a kitchen table, but a more careful inspection revealed the truth. The table was actually Dad's cement mixer turned upright with a piece of plywood balanced on the rounded opening. A red-checkered tablecloth and vase with wildflowers camouflaged the now convenient inconvenience.

Once again masters of their domain, they invited me to join them for high tea. We dined on crustless peanut butter sandwiches while sipping perfectly sweetened sun tea. They eventually invited Dad to share the cuisine.

That was my family in DeGraff. I remember us as being typically normal most of the time. When I was with my friends and their families, I knew deep down how fortunate I was to be in mine. Although there was nothing wrong with my friends' families, they simply did not seem as special as ours. Some of us are born lucky and graced with childhood memories that last a lifetime. My memories are always welcomed, but they are appreciated even more during life's bleakest moments. I found myself trapped in one of those moments now.

Shaking the snow from my head, I turned away from the university's guesthouse and my mother's Queen Anne. I ran frozen-cold numb through the slush to our home where, fumbling my key, I was unable to unlock the front door. In my frustration, I planted my thumb against the doorbell and did not let up as the two-tone ring echoed again and again and again. When Sherée finally opened the door, I was shivering uncontrollably. As soon as I was inside, I blurted out Kurt's urgent words about Mom.

Sherée took charge, preparing a hot bath and helping me out of my damp clothes. While I soaked in the steaming water, she made airline reservations. We packed quickly and left for Little Rock to spend the night before our early morning flight to Tucson. For the first time in my life, I was not looking forward to visiting my family.

PART II

Chapter Six
COWBOYS

Friday, December 5th

I was unable to sleep that night at the Comfort Inn Suites beside Little Rock's airport. Okay, I probably slept a little. When someone tells me they didn't sleep a wink, my antennae of suspicion shoot up. But I honestly do not remember sleeping. I missed the travel pillows I forgot in our haste to leave, and I was rendered an insomniac by the synthetic sack of stiffness the motel supplied. Sherée slept soundly and arose refreshed while I grumbled up, tired and agitated. Sensing my mood, she kept to herself as we readied ourselves for the long day ahead. It wasn't until our short shuttle drive to the airport that I finally spoke in real sentences.

"I hope the flights are on time," I muttered. "I hate flying through Chicago, particularly in the dead of winter. We are always delayed."

41

"I hope they are, too. But if they aren't, we will make the best of it. Do I finally get my morning kiss?"

Sherée takes assertive charge on flight days, as airports and their security clearances intimidate me. Fortunately, we were graced to have a chipper and witty gate attendant who helped our check-in go smoothly. I sensed that just maybe our trip would be uneventful. And it was—until Chicago. Upon exiting the plane at O'Hare, we immediately glanced up at the departure monitors and read the dreaded news: the connecting flight to Tucson was delayed for more than an hour. After we found a place to sit down, Sherée dug out a puzzle book from her carry-on bag. I sat next to her, mumbling some unintelligible words while folding my arms tightly in front of me. My wife will tell you that it's my classic perturbative posture.

I eventually relaxed a bit and leaned over to kiss Sherée on the cheek. Resigned to accept our fate, I echoed the words she'd spoken earlier. "We will make the best of it."

Having inherited from Mom a fascination for people watching, I began observing the hundreds of passengers hurrying by. I noticed a little boy sitting across from us and guessed him to be about six or seven years old. He was wearing a sweatshirt, pants, and stocking cap all bearing the insignia of the Dallas Cowboys. He grinned at me, and I smiled back before affirming the obvious.

"I see you like the Cowboys."

His reply was animated. "No, sir, I don't *like* 'em. I *love* 'em! Don't you?"

I believe we inherit, through an unspilled blood oath, a loyalty for our fathers' favorite teams. For his lifetime, Dad cheered for everything Detroit, particularly the Lions and Tigers. Hence, I've always been an avid Detroit Lions fan.

The young Cowboys fan had asked me a question I was hesitant to answer. No, I was not a lover of the Cowboys, and until we moved to Arkansas, I must admit I often rooted against them. Since most of my Arkansas friends are Dallas fans, I have become less vociferous in expressing my true feelings. Out of respect for this peewee fan, however, I decided to tell a small white lie. Besides, the Cowboys' owner, Jerry Jones, is from Arkansas, so I suppose I'm obligated to like them a little, right? "Sure, of course I'm a fan, who isn't?"

He bounced excitedly over to high-five me, but his mother quickly halted our little celebration with a sharp, "Bobbie Lee, stop bothering the gentleman." Although I wanted to explain that he wasn't bothering me, and was actually a pleasant distraction, I thought better about contradicting her. Bobbie Lee listened to his mother and became engrossed in Velcroing and re-Velcroing his Cowboys tennis shoes, a repetitive action I am guessing he hoped would cause me to notice his footwear. I did and gave him a "those are pretty cool" thumbs up.

While watching him, I was struck by the difference in his cowboy outfit from mine at his age. Back then I had the real deal Western garb—authentic hat, flannel shirt, bandana, denim jeans, boots, and the mandatory strapped-on six-shooter. John Slater, my classmate and neighbor two houses down for all of our DeGraff years, also wore legitimate duds, and we'd play cowboys and Indians (we were not as culturally sensitive back then as we should have been) from dawn till dusk.

We had great fun in our portrayals of the white-hatted good guys, especially John. John always cast himself as the lead cowboy, while I was relegated to sidekick status. We played all the heroic cowboy duos: Gene Autry and Pat Buttram (me with a nasal voice), Hopalong Cassidy and Edgar Buchanan (me with a raspy voice), Wild Bill Hickok and Jingles (me with a high-pitched voice), The Cisco Kid and Pancho (me with an accent), Marshal Matt Dillon and Deputy Chester Goode (me with a limp), and The Lone Ranger and Tonto (me with a feather).

I balked, however, at being Dale Evans to John's Roy Rogers, but I did agree for one humiliating afternoon to be Bullet, Roy's ever faithful, run-along-beside-him canine. I managed to prance on all fours for a few paces, then regained enough dignity to become DeGraff's lone two-legged barker.

Although our small town could not boast of being home to any honest-to-goodness cowboys, David Downing came pretty darn close, at least by our modest west central Ohioan standards. David worked at the DeGraff Stockyards and Meat Packing Company, and through my idyllic little boy eyes, he was as near to cowboy-worthy as we could manage. David qualified because he wrangled cattle daily and chased pigs to their pork-chopped demise.

I seldom saw David Downing without his cheek stuffed full of Mail Pouch Chewing Tobacco. No one else I knew chewed tobacco. He was a master chewer and spitter, hitting objects as far away as ten feet with accuracy. Had there been an Olympic event for tobacco spitting, David could have represented DeGraff and the nation with pride.

He was a hero to me not only as a cowboy, but in the world of romance as well. By dating a girl from Bellefontaine, the largest city in Logan County, he was also one of DeGraff's leading men when it came to the department of love. To step across our borders and venture into Bellefontaine territory to woo one of the big city gals required a feat of unparalleled nerve. I looked up to him and admired his confidence. He plucked his lady right out from under the noses of those hapless Bellefontaine guys and brought her to the DeGraff Roxie Theater for Saturday night movies. Even though Bellefontaine had a modern movie house, the Holland Movie Theatre, David chose to come back home. I guess the Roxie was cozier, or maybe he was just showing off DeGraff. I didn't know his reason but was glad for it.

The Roxie was only open on Friday and Saturday nights, and tradition called for Friday showings to be attended by adults with Saturdays reserved for kids. I'm not certain how that custom began, but it was strictly adhered to throughout all of my years in DeGraff. Even though David had grown dangerously close to adulthood, no one questioned his Saturday night attendance at the theatre. In fact we welcomed it and his entrance.

Just before Angelina Gutella, who operated the Roxie with assistance from her first-generation Italian brother Angelo, dimmed the lights for the pre-movie cartoon, David would make his confident, high-in-the-saddle appearance. And oh my goodness, what an appearance it was. The thrill of watching him stride down the Roxie's worn-out red carpet with his belle from Bellefontaine made my twenty-five cent admission fee worth the cost. He was always dressed to the cowboy nines in a sequin-studded black silk shirt, meticulously pressed Levi's, pant legs rolled to reveal highly polished snakeskin boots, a red polka-dot bandana tied loosely around the neck, and a perfectly shaped white felt Stetson hat perched atop his slicked-back pompadour.

But my real focus week after week was on the Bellefontaine girl locked tightly to his arm. She was a knockout. David even had the good manners to leave his Mail Pouch stowed at home, validating just how much respect he had for his date. In my pre-pubescent mind, this no-tobacco gesture represented true love.

The two of them always sat in the third row on the left, and David stood until she was seated. Then he'd slowly untie the bandana, wave it three times like a waiter in a fine restaurant preparing the napkin for a patron's lap, and drape it on the empty seat beside him. Carefully, very carefully, he'd remove his cowboy hat and rest it on the bandana. When the lights dimmed and the cartoon began to roll across the screen, he'd sit down. At that point he was on his own, and I would stop staring at him and his date. Watching any longer would have been impolite.

How I envied David's dating success! I wanted to seek him out for manly advice, and I almost did. While I was delivering the daily newspaper one afternoon, we met on the sidewalk in front of the Morris Rexall Drugstore where he bought his chew.

Unfortunately, I became so engrossed by how accurately he spat squirts of tobacco on the fire hydrant, I forgot my question. I simply watched in amazement like a little squirt myself.

When I was a kid, I worshiped a number of cowboy heroes. But none stood taller nor enthralled me more than David Downing. I lost track of him after we left DeGraff and moved to Kent. I hope he married his Bellefontaine girl, settled down, and raised a corral of little cowpokes. Happy trails to you, David!

Bobbie Lee had fallen asleep, scrunched down as close to his mother as the intrusive armrest would allow. When their flight was announced, his mother gently tousled his hair to wake him, and he glanced over at me to wave a half-asleep goodbye. I waved back and said, "Take care, Cowboy. Good luck to your team." Hand-in-hand with his mom, he disappeared into the crowd.

We were not as fortunate. Our flight had been delayed again, this time for ninety more annoying minutes. I resigned myself to O'Hare's curse and decided Bobbie Lee's nap might be a good idea for me as well. I snuggled as close to Sherée as possible, and she tousled my hair like I was a little boy, too. "Get some rest, sweets," she said. "I'll keep track of our departure."

I usually find it difficult to sleep in public and decided simply closing my eyes would be enough. I recaptured the picture of Bobbie Lee and his mother holding hands while maneuvering their way through the crowded airport. Mothers remain their children's security blankets for life, somehow managing to keep ahold of their hands in spite of passing years and separating miles. With floating images of Bobbie Lee and his mother intermingling with recollections of me and my mother, I felt little-boy secure again. Even within the intrusiveness of strangers around me, I slowly and softly drifted back.

When we lived in Oberlin and Dad attended the Conservatory of Music, his classes were during the day and into early evening. Because I was an only child at the time, I occupied most of my mother's attention. We lived in a small, two-bedroom house just off campus. I don't remember much about the house except for our living room, dominated by Dad's prized possession—a battered yet functional Wurlitzer upright piano given to him by his mother. He was proud of the piano because both she and he had learned to play on it.

One of my carefully preserved memories that survived the Oberlin years involves Dad playing the Wurlitzer at night after supper and Mom singing. Although I think they had a respectable repertoire of musical selections, I really remember only one song, "The Band Played On." During life's quiet moments, I am able to clear my mind of accumulated trivialities and hear Dad's perfectly keyed notes accompanying Mom's sweet soprano voice. With just the right amount of concentration, I see Dad standing up from the piano bench and taking Mom into his arms. The two of them would dance to the music of their a cappella voices.

> *Casey would waltz with a strawberry blonde*
> *and the band played on.*
> *He'd glide 'cross the floor*
> *with the girl he adored*
> *and the band played on.*

I never tire of replaying that magical moment from a young son's past. Never.

Another Oberlin memory involves my mother doing the ironing, a weekly chore she disliked. Every Thursday morning, Mom would haul the cumbersome ironing board into our living room with me following behind, lugging an anvil-like Westinghouse steam iron. Together, we'd then carry the laundry basket filled with freshly laundered clothes, each crumpled item awaiting its weekly pressing and transformation back to respectable wearability.

Mom was meticulous about the way she ironed Dad's shirts and pants. His clothes received regal treatment because as a WWII veteran and married man, he was a role model for his younger classmates. When she was done, she'd carefully place the pressed masterpieces on hangers and hand them to me to return to the bedroom closet. I'd stand on one of the chairs from our kitchen table and stretch almost beyond my reach to secure the hangers on the closet's metal bar. I savored the danger of my duty.

After the other clothes were ironed, folded, and placed carefully back in the laundry basket, Mom and I would carry it to the bedrooms and refill empty dresser drawers. We both felt a sense of accomplishment when the task was finished. Best of all, I could barely wait for our ritual of celebration—a series of happy kisses on the cheek and an in-unison shout of "Yippee hi ho the cowboys!"

I do not know the reason for shouting "Yippee hi ho the cowboys" and never thought to ask. The words simply felt pure and natural. I do know I was happy because my mother was happy, and I felt good because she felt good. Good and happy moments such as these are to be relished.

Our tradition followed me into adulthood. During special occasions for grand celebration, I revive the unabashed, unashamed exuberance of a small boy and his mother, although I now silently chant "Yippee hi ho the cowboys" to myself.

"Rick, wake up, people are looking at you. You keep repeating, 'Yippee hi ho, yippee hi ho.' Were you dreaming?"

"Yeah, I guess I was … I guess I was dreaming." I wanted to float back to childhood, my mother, and ironing day, but Sherée was insistent.

"Hurry up, we need to get a move on. They've just announced our flight is boarding."

I grabbed our carry-on bags and fast-paced with Sherée to the gate. I thought about shouting "Yippee hi ho the cowboys" for the other delayed passengers to hear but wisely resisted the temptation. Airport security tends to be intolerant of strange behavior.

Heroes

For decades I tended
to swap my fading heroes
for flashy new ones.
The practice began in youth
and grew with me.
Older now,
I have
more respect for
tradition.
The past
has its place,
and my childhood heroes
are back home
for good.

COWBOY: Sunset Carson was the best.
POLICEMAN: Dick Tracy always got his man.
ATHLETE: Al Kaline, silky smooth in right field.
ACTOR: Humphrey Bogart, here's looking at you.
TEACHER: Miss Betsy McGee, the grammar queen.
COMPOSER: Ludwig van Beethoven, the master of masters.
POET: Robert Frost never forced a rhyme.
NOVELIST: J.D. Salinger, the enigmatic one.
PRESIDENT: JFK, still mourned.
PARENTS: Forever.

What happens when
Mom and Dad
are gone?
Real heroes
happen by
just
once.

Chapter Seven
SIMPLIFICATION

I relaxed during the flight to Tucson, knowing it was a much-appreciated respite from what awaited us. Sherée was relaxed, too, having fallen asleep next to me before the plane even lifted off the runway. I felt at peace as I gazed at the scene outside my window. The remarkable skyscape was gowned in infinite blue and accessorized with white layers of whipped cream puffiness. I appreciate life's quiet pauses, those rare inter-missions in which I am able to lose myself. They do not happen often enough. Sherée and I live a hectic pace, and that makes meditative moments such as these true treasures.

The flight was especially pleasant because no babies cried and no restless kids kicked at my seat back or pounded on their tray tables. If I owned an airline, I'd eliminate first class and coach, and replace them with adult class and children confinement. And I would serve pizza to everyone.

I glanced around the cabin and slowly realized I was the only passenger not sleeping or reading or listening to an electronic gadget plugged into my ears. I was the flight anomaly. Laptops, DVD players, headsets, and insidious gaming gadgets had hijacked the plane. I felt overpowered by the newest generation of electronics, an aggressive genus that seems to evolve annually into things that always promise better and smaller, but are only more complicated. Quite frankly, they scare me, and I often pine for my obsolete four-track tape player with its easy to manage push buttons.

When did everything get so complicated? Well, here's one answer—the advent of a computer age that pledged more free time and simpler lives. Ha! I literally bought into the charade and continue to pay heavily. Vacations are just another place to check e-mail. Slapped by that sudden downer of a thought, I lapsed into worrying about how many e-mails I must have accumulated even in the short time we'd been gone. I worried about when I'd have time to respond, which ones were urgent and... I nursed down a calming breath. Sherée was still asleep, and the window beckoned me back. I returned to the view and thought about the question again. When *did* everything get so complicated?

Blaming the computer age is too harsh. Other culprits contribute. Life's complexities take root after college graduation: the first job, real responsibilities, marriage, mortgage, and money management. Things grow even more complicated as we try to share equal time with parents and in-laws who are separated from us by hundreds and sometimes thousands of miles. Let's be honest. There is too much technology, too much information, and too much invasiveness, all resulting in too little privacy. As a consequence, life is complicated. Ah, but I have developed a homegrown remedy to counteract the revolution. I have my own escape route to safe havens.

I float back to bicycle rides along the scenic back roads surrounding my small hometown. I daydream the welcoming downhill slopes and coast effortlessly while using no hands, gliding carefree.

I rediscover the joys of what used to be. Their discovery separates me from minutiae, protects me from mayhem, and saves me from the mundane.

I drift easily. The past has its place, and I like that place. I savor the old and relish reflecting on it. I peel back time, peel back layers, peel back remembrances to revive favorite memories and breathe them back to life. I write favorite memories and read them after a bad day. I read them again after other bad days. I capture more memories, write more memories, reread more memories, capture more, write more . . . write more . . . write . . .

Sherée continued to slumber beside me, and I couldn't reach my notebook in the carry-on without waking her. I hoped I would remember my thoughts. I sometimes do not. I signaled the flight attendant and asked for more hot tea and biscotti cookies. Life again simplified, and I felt ready to welcome what was before me.

Simplify Life

See the world through a child's eyes. Pay attention like one who is experiencing wonderment for the first time.

Identify the positive. Nurture the positive and isolate the negative.

Memorize a favorite poem. When stressed, repeat the poem like a mantra.

Play classical music. Become intoxicated by the magic of the masters.

Look back for comfort. Recalling the old is as gratifying as exploring the new.

Imagine pleasant thoughts. Save happy thoughts and discard sad ones.

Find a favorite teacher. Teachers delight in being remembered.

Yield to the local's allure. Discover the local before trekking to distant places.

Leave work at work. Prioritize the real priorities at home with family.

Invest in community service. Complexities dissolve while serving others.

Focus on life's satisfiers. Explore the things that bring satisfaction.

Enjoy the quiet of evening. Pajamas on by 8:00 p.m. to rest in an easy chair with a petted cat purring in lapped comfort. The murmuring rhythms echo simplicity in its *purrest* form.

S I M P L I F Y   L I F E

Chapter Eight

SHALL WE DANCE?

I must have fallen asleep. The captain's announcement, "Flight attendants, please prepare the cabin for landing," startled me, and I instinctively moved my seat to the upright position without being told. Sherée sleeps through anything, and I let her continue for a few more minutes.

I looked outside in anticipation of one of my favorite window seat views—the descent into Tucson. Four separate mountain ranges fortress together to protect the vast terrain of housing developments, high-rises, and the intersecting roadways sand-boxing the sprawling desert. One positive from our late arrival, several hours past the originally scheduled afternoon touchdown, was my chance to see Tucson lit up in nocturnal splendor. From the air, the pageant is prismatic. I enjoyed the sight momentarily before soberly remembering the reason for our visit. As I slouched back against my seat, the scene outside my window blurred to a dim haze. I turned to Sherée and gently squeezed her hand to comfort me and awaken her.

Sherée called Kurt after we landed, and we agreed to meet in baggage claim. As I listened to her talking to him, I had a vision of us standing beside an empty carousel, its conveyer belt winding endlessly as we watched for non-arriving bags. For no logical reason, I sometimes create situations to worry about, but there was no need for worry this time. Not only was Kurt waiting for us, he already had our bags beside him. After quick but deep hugs, I asked the question I'd been dreading an answer to since yesterday's telephone conversation with him. "How is Mom?"

Kurt paused a little too long for my comfort, then answered solemnly. "Not well, Rick, not well at all. Even with her oxygen increased to the maximum, she struggles to breathe. Now that the two of you are here, maybe she will perk up."

"What about Dad?"

This time he answered quickly. "You know Dad, always the optimist. He seems to be in denial and unable to accept just how bad she is this time. Not only has there been no mention of dying, Dad is talking about taking her home."

Kurt led us to the car parked in the far reaches of a well-lit section and remote-opened the trunk to Dad's recently purchased white Dodge Intrepid. After I stowed our suitcases, I noticed several ugly scrapes on the passenger side rear bumper and along the lower panel. The scratches were tattooed with swaths of bright yellow paint.

"What happened here?" I asked while fingering the scars.

"I was with Dad when he did it. We were rushing Mom to the emergency room, and he panicked while trying to back into a parking space. He maneuvered the car forward and back, not realizing he was rubbing against the cement base of a light pole. I could hear the dull grinding sound and yelled for him to stop, but he wasn't paying attention to his parking or to me. He kept turning the wheel and scraping against the base. After I grabbed his hand, he stopped. I guess he was focused on Mom and getting her inside. He still hasn't seen the damage."

Kurt drove, and we small-talked jobs and weather until we reached the University Medical Center. We'd passed the facility many times during our previous visits to Tucson, but I'd never been inside. Kurt parked the wounded Intrepid, and on our walk to the main entrance, he pointed out Dad's cement base victim. His car's white paint blended awkwardly with the stanchion's once-yellow finish. The fracas had done neither any good.

When Kurt said Mom was on the fourth floor in Room 424, I asked him if we could take the stairs instead of using an elevator. I needed the extra time to prepare myself. No matter how desperate a situation is, as the eldest son I have always felt pressured to present a composed decorum when it involves my parents or brothers. I've never asked if it really matters.

We climbed the stairs to the fourth floor and followed Kurt along the sterile hallway to Mom's room. When we entered, Dad and Jeff looked relieved. Mom, however, was obviously startled. My mother has always taken the lead in any conversation, and her lying pale and weak while attached to ominous bags of fluid, electronic monitors, and a nasal cannula providing robust doses of oxygen did not interfere with her leading this one.

"Rick, why are you here? And Sherée? What's going on? Am I that sick?"

As I bent down to kiss her cheek, two thin intraveneoused arms stretched around me to complete a soft hug. I stepped back to examine her more closely. She had reduced to finely wrinkled parchment covering frail bones and looked so much worse than she had just two months before when she and Dad left Clarksville for Arizona. Her breathing was labored and at a quicker pace, the hospital's oxygen forcing into her more aggressively than her portable machine was able to. I tried not to appear shocked.

"Yes, Mom, you are sick. You have not been getting enough oxygen, but that's not why Sherée and I are here. We came because we haven't seen you since October." Some untruths are appropriate.

Suspicious, she countered me. "But why now? It's almost three weeks before my birthday and the holidays. Why are you in Tucson now?"

"Because we wanted to come, and we plan to stay until after the New Year."

Doubt added a small splash of color to her pallid face. "Can you really stay that long? How could you have that much vacation time, honey?"

"Certainly I can stay that long. Remember, I am the president after all. Presidents can do that kind of stuff."

My mother spent much of her life wary of educators in authoritative positions—principals, superintendents, deans, and presidents—until I crossed over and became one of them. I think she learned her suspicions honestly from Dad who, although an exceptional teacher and always respectful toward his bosses, seldom let their priorities get in the way of his.

She appreciated my response. "Of course, you can be gone for as long as you want. After all, you are the president!"

A nurse came into the room to remind us that visiting hours were about over. While the others queued up for their goodnights to Mom, I seized eldest son control. I had a plan. Admittedly, I had not cleared my plan with anyone, not even Sherée, but it was a fine one nonetheless.

"All of you look exhausted, especially you, Dad. I'm going to spend the night with Mom. I can sleep in one of the waiting rooms. You go home, get some rest, and come back tomorrow. Sherée is staying at Kurt's."

Everyone must have been tired because no one argued with me, and that was unusual, particularly for Sherée because we never sleep apart. After assuring Mom she'd be okay for one night without Dad, I walked my family to the elevator. Sherée asked if I was positive I didn't want her to stay with me. I promised

I would be fine on my own. I think I meant it, even though a shiver of uncertainty ran through me as the elevator doors shut. I waited a moment to calm myself before going back to Mom.

I entered her room quietly in hopes she'd fallen asleep. She hadn't, although she looked extremely tired. I tried to kiss her goodnight and leave, but that was not about to happen. She was ready for conversation and swallowed large gulps of air to prepare herself.

"Rick, I'm glad you are staying. I've been thinking about you lately. I still worry about you. I know I shouldn't, but I do. Moms are supposed to worry, right?"

I smiled at her. "Yeah, Mom, worry has always been a major part of your job description."

She turned her head slightly and adjusted the cannula. The hum of oxygen pumping into her sounded louder within the room's quiet.

"I've also been thinking about DeGraff. I believe those years were our best ones as a family. We made so many friends and had such fun. All of my memories are good ones. The same for you?"

I nodded in agreement as she realigned the cannula once again. I cringed watching her struggle and didn't know what to say. More humming and tugging filled the long pause as she battled for breath. This time she won.

"Guess what I was talking about with your father this morning."

"What, Mom?"

"Do you remember the time we made you take dance lessons with us? The lessons were in Bellefontaine at the Arthur Murray Dance Studio. I believe you were in the sixth or seventh grade."

Of course I remembered. How could I forget that experience? "No, I was in the fifth grade."

She moved her hand to her mouth. It was a common gesture she often made when she was collecting words for just the right comment. She removed her hand only after the words were captured. "Well, I've never told you this, but your father and I felt bad for putting you through that. The lessons were really for us, your dad and me, but we made you go also. I cannot for the life of me remember the reason we were so insistent. We never forced lessons on Jeff or Kurt, but we did on you. I cannot imagine why."

I, however, clearly remembered their reason, but it was too late at night to venture into that long story. I decided to save it for another time. "Well, being the oldest son has its advantages and disadvantages," I said to her. "But, you know something? Years later, I now consider those dance lessons to have been a definite advantage. I'm glad you were insistent."

She looked relieved, almost as though a decades-old weight had been lifted. Even her next few breaths didn't seem quite as labored. "Good. Then I'm glad we were insistent, too."

"Okay, no more worries about the past. We have more immediate concerns to deal with, like you getting better, and that begins with you going to sleep. I will be down the hallway if you need me." I kissed her forehead, and we promised we would see each other in the morning. I remember hoping she'd be able to keep her half of the promise.

The waiting room was a short distance down the hallway, and, thankfully, no one else had decided to spend the night there. I was looking forward to being alone. I tested three couches and one cushy-looking chair before choosing a small sofa. I found myself staring at a Ron Popeil infomercial hawking at me from the wall-mounted television in the far corner. The ubiquitous Ron was pitching another one of his creative inventions, this time the Pocket Fisherman, a miniature fishing pole designed to fold in half and fit in a back pocket. As a kid, I would have begged my parents to let me buy one with my paper route money.

It would have been perfect for fishing in the Bokenghelas Creek that trickled through the pasture behind our house in DeGraff.

The nurse who reminded us about visiting hours walked by the door, and I jumped up to see if she could turn off the television. Before getting the remote, she asked if I was spending the night. When I answered yes, she offered to find a pillow and blanket for me. Southern hospitality was alive and well in Tucson.

Although I was tired, I found it difficult to fall asleep. I was still staring at the ticking wall clock when its big and little hands found one another for the stroke of midnight. The fact that my body was set on Arkansas time didn't help either. But what really kept me from sleeping was the image of my mother lying nearby on what could very well be her deathbed. I tried to force that picture from my mind by replacing it with far more pleasant thoughts.

The idea of Mom and Dad lamenting my dance lessons made me chuckle, and I started recalling our lively sessions. From there, I found my mental escape route back to DeGraff, fifth grade, school classmates, dance music, the box step, small talk...and Eloise.

Chapter Nine
PHILIP ROHRER

Philip Rohrer could really dance. If he had challenged Bobby in a "dance off" to be Cissy's new partner on *The Lawrence Welk Show*, Bobby would have had to cut a finer rug to keep Cissy and his job. Philip Rohrer was that good.

He and his family lived on a farm close to Wimpy Knight's property in Logansville, DeGraff's little cousin two miles to the north. Like Ned Heintz, Philip was my classmate. Unlike Ned, Philip did not aspire to spend his life on the family farm. His parents and his older sister Patsy encouraged him to pursue other interests, and he excelled in everything but sports. After graduating from college, he worked as a cameraman on Ruth Lyons' program, *The 50/50 Club*, in Cincinnati. Ruth Lyons was known throughout Ohio because of her highly successful television program, and Philip soon became her favorite cameraman and our singular DeGraff celebrity.

Philip, who played snare drum in Dad's concert and marching bands, was an incredible musician with uncanny rhythmic instincts. We lower brass players sat directly in front of the percussion section, positioning me perfectly to enjoy his frequent riffs. Every once in a while, what he played was actually written on the score, but most of the time Philip improvised.

At first my dad did not appreciate his extemporaneous flourishes, but he finally came around to accept Philip's unique abilities. Dad even tried to claim he was the one who taught Philip how to play the drums, but we all knew the truth. Philip was simply a natural. When we were freshmen, Dad gave in completely and asked Philip to teach the other percussionists a few of his cadences. As a conductor, my father seldom went off script, but Philip's remarkable musical talents made him the exception.

Yes, Philip Rohrer had an amazing talent, and his instincts for rhythm set him apart from the rest of us, especially his moves as a dancer. I saw his prowess on display for the first time during a fifth and sixth grade mixer, which was a kind of pre-prom for upper-elementary students.

We had played a basketball game earlier in the day—fifth grade versus sixth—in front of both classes, and I had made the winning shot (it still ranks among my greatest athletic achievements) to clinch our hotly contested underdog victory. We won seven to six. The sixth grade players continued to seethe about our monumental upset, so we fifth grade boys massed closely together for safety before the mixer. Fortunately, the dance was held in the school cafeteria and not the gymnasium. I say "fortunately" because Bobbie Bixler, a giant at five feet, eight inches among the sixth grade almost-men, challenged us to a rematch right then and there. Since custodian Lawrence Linet had already cleaned and locked up the gym for the night, Bobbie's incessant "let's play another one" double-dog dares were chanted in vain.

The rectangular cafeteria was dance-size perfect, and even roomier after Lawrence removed most of the tables and placed the metal folding chairs along both sides of the cafeteria's long, grey walls. The school's state-of-the-art hi-fi record player stacked high with 45s sat ready to perform at one end, while four tables loaded with two large punch bowls and tempting trays of cellophane-wrapped chocolate chip and peanut butter cookies occupied the opposite end.

The sixth grade girls were responsible for decorating the cafeteria. Mrs. Strayer, the art teacher for all grade levels elementary through high school, generously provided sheets of red and blue construction paper, our school colors. The girls' cleverly crafted creations hung from fluorescent light fixtures and along the windows, walls, and refreshment tables. Only one bank of lights was left on, giving the room a warm and inviting glow. I liked it. This certainly didn't look like the place where we ravenously wolfed down food every school day.

The dance was scheduled to start at seven o'clock. As the cafeteria clock ticked to the exact second of that precise moment, sixth grade teacher Mr. Claude Bailey whistled. All chatter ceased. Even we naïve fifth graders, under the tutelage of our teacher, Mrs. Curl, knew the strictly obeyed Claude Bailey Whistle Rule. When he whistles, everyone quiets to drop-dead silence. His whistle still remains the shrillest one I have ever heard. Rumor was he once whistled so loudly in the school parking lot that a freight train traveling full speed through DeGraff slammed on its brakes, the conductor convinced he'd heard the emergency system's alarm. Unbelievable, yes, but in DeGraff with nothing much going on, rumors lived long and died hard.

I was digging something out of my right ear with an index finger when Bailey whistled. As trained, I stood motionless as a statue, my finger still firmly planted in my ear. I had no intention of removing it until he finished speaking. He definitely did not need a microphone or megaphone as he bellowed our orders for the evening.

"Ladies and gentlemen, boys and girls, welcome to this year's fifth and sixth grade mixer. Listen carefully to what I am about to say. Mrs. Curl and I expect all of you, and that is each and every one of you without exception, to be on your best behavior, to be respectful and courteous, to act like you have some common sense, to dance in a civilized manner, to keep your shoes and socks on, to thank your partner at the end of each dance, to eat no more than four cookies, to drink only two glasses of punch, to not loiter in the dark corners, and to ask Mrs. Curl or me if you need to leave the cafeteria for a bathroom break. Are there any questions?" *Who dared to speak?* "Okay then, have fun!"

After Mr. Bailey concluded his declaration of our dependence, Ned Heintz slapped me on the back of the head. "Hey, Goober, I think you can pull your finger out of your ear now. What were you doing, half listening?" I half laughed. We found a seat together by Frog Comer and John Slater, and were soon joined by Philip Rohrer, Charles Tamplin, Paul Whitehead, Bill Ward, and Wendell Stevenson. After Paul Jenny, Bob Donald, Jerry Beatty, Lynn Shultz, and the rest of the guys wedged in, we were squeezed into our half of the fifth-grade side tighter than Fats Domino's waistband. I looked down the row and saw mother hen Skinner Hittepole gathering our female classmates to sit along the other half. Gender segregation thrived in fifth grade back then and probably still does.

On the opposite side of the room, Mr. Bailey was commandeering his sixth grade squadron into a boy/girl seating arrangement. When Ned noticed the commingled alignment, he howled, "Holy cow, look at what Bailey is doing to those poor slobs! I hope Curly doesn't follow his lead." Mrs. Curl did not, and we boys remained safely separated from the girls. As soon as both classes were formally seated, we began to eyeball each other from across the room, kind of like Yankees and Confederates sizing up one another before a battle. Mrs. Curl turned on the record player, lowered its needled arm, and the music flowed. I was so nervous that any number would have done me in, but

Bill Haley and His Comets belting out "Rock Around the Clock" sealed my doom. Fast dances tormented me.

Seconds into the song, my hands started trembling as my lower lip twitched. After a few more beats, I began to feel nauseous and looked frantically for Mr. Bailey or Mrs. Curl so I could request permission to exit. It was barely 7:05 p.m., and I was already a no-rockin'-around-this-clock mess!

I guess all of us were nervous about dancing because no one ventured onto the floor. Then the most extraordinary thing happened. Philip Rohrer gallantly arose from his chair, glided down to our row's female-only section, and asked Susie Koogler to dance. They stepped to the center of the room in supreme confidence, bowed to one another, and danced like nothing I'd ever seen, not even on *Lawrence Welk*. They were in perfect beat, perfect melody, perfect harmony—they were in perfect everything! I was stunned, amazed, and to be honest, downright envious. I couldn't take my eyes off them as they jittered like jitterbugs jitterbugging across a rippleless pond at twilight, satin sleek and summer breeze effortless.

Skinner Hittepole, Carol Jean Cox, Rita Thornton, and Cat Taylor scrambled onto the floor to join them, followed by Kay Schmidt, Linda Dunlap, JoAnn Carpenter, Arlene Hurley, and Judy Kaeck. Next came a bevy of sixth-grade girls led by Diane Schlumbohm, Janice Madden, and Patty Krisher. Close behind were Joyce Hengsteler, Betty Perk, Nathalea Wical, and Marilyn Jackson. Surrounded by a harem of wiggling, gigging, dance-till-they-drop admirers, Philip quickened his pace to accommodate each one.

Just as Bill Haley and his crew chimed *"five, six, and seven,"* Paul Whitehead jumped up and shouted, "Boys, out there is the promised land. Philip has far more than he can handle. I'm primed and ready. Watch these moves!" I slumped down further into my chair, then crept up wide-eyed and gape-mouthed as Paul whirled toward the dancing mass.

Geez, he could dance, too! Who was teaching these guys? Paul's technique was far different from Philip's. Paul was the best natural athlete in our class, and because of his athleticism, he was a leg-stomping, power-pounding, shifty-moving Gene Kelly type. Philip Rohrer was the opposite. Lithe and slender, he was nimble and soft bouncing, a cat-like Fred Astaire. If Philip was grace, Paul was grind.

The end of the song ended their dancing. We guys didn't talk or look at one another as Philip and Paul strode back to their chairs. Throat dry and tongue numbed, I couldn't have spoken if I'd wanted to. After several seconds of wordlessness, Ned Heintz finally asked the question we were all thinking. "Gosh, fellas, where did you learn to dance like that?"

Paul mumbled something about an older cousin. Philip spoke clearly, and I remember his answer verbatim. "Man, you don't learn how to dance. You feel the music running through your body and move to it." Yeah, I remember what he said. But it meant nothing to my body or me.

The next three numbers were slow ones, and except for Philip and Paul, the rest of us boys stayed planted in our rowed seats like a farmer's crop of summer sweet corn. Mr. Bailey had seen enough. He turned off the record player, shrill-whistled, and sternly announced, "All right ladies and gentlemen, boys and girls, the next dance will be a Sadie Hawkins. Ladies, you invite the gentlemen to dance."

Rats, could this get any worse? I could not dance, did not want to dance, and would refuse any offers to dance. That was that, and I vowed to stand my ground while staying seated. Nothing could change my mind. Well, almost nothing.

Prom Swanson, the goddess of the sixth grade, arose from her chair from across the room and began heading our way. Prom Swanson was the fantasy of every guy I knew, including the big boys in junior high. She was a definite dazzler. I once got her attention by crowding in line in front of her at the school's drinking fountain. She poked me in the back, called me a weasel, and announced that I needed to get my rear-end back in line. I happily obeyed and floated on air for days after that. Prom Swanson had touched me!

I leered like a stalker as she approached our side, rejoicing at each feminine step. Everything but Prom blurred to fuzziness. Nothing moved but Prom. I stopped breathing, not wanting to distract my focus. She was looking our way. Was she looking at me? In anticipation I prepared a dance acceptance speech.

"Why of course, Prom, I will be honored to dance with you. How charming of you to ask. You are looking unusually divine this evening." Good, great, perfect.

As she swept closer, I tried to stand but my legs were like Jell-O. *Please, legs, don't betray me now!* She was almost in front of me. I crept up one inch, one more inch, another, and then another. I was squatting slightly above the chair and begging my legs to keep lifting me up. *C'mon, legs, help me stand up!* My dream girl was oh so close. I ran the speech through my head again. Still perfect. And then she stopped, rolled her eyes, and said, "Sit down, weasel. You think I want to dance with you? You've got to be kidding. I'm here for Philip."

Crushed, squished, stomped, flattened, pummeled, pulverized. Yep, I was a pathetic, broken little man. I tried to breathe, but my nasal cavities had collapsed. My jaw locked tight and forced my mouth to stay closed. My heart was pounding harder and faster. The room corkscrewed, and I started to wobble backwards. I was about to faint! As I crumpled into the chair, my head slammed against the wall—THUD—shot forward, and banged back again. I sucked in a deep breath as I faced the galling truth: I was an idiot. How in any stretch of even my wild imagination could I think Prom Swanson would want to dance with me when dance king Philip was revved up and in gear? Some realities are undeniable at any age.

Brokenhearted and completely deflated, I didn't dance once

that entire evening. But I did manage to scoop up eight cookies, right in front of Bailey and Curl, and washed them down with four chugged glasses of punch. I sulked away from the table and loitered alone in one of the darkened corners until Mrs. Curl asked me to return to my seat.

During breakfast the following morning, my parents asked the inevitable "how was the dance?" question. Even as a lowly fifth grader, I had learned the art of evasiveness when faced with Mom and Pop inquiries, especially if the line of questioning involved little Rickie's personal life. Unfortunately, news traveled fast in DeGraff, our small town wired for the Internet decades before its invention. Since Dad was well connected, he and Mom were bound to hear about my non-dance-at-the-dance disaster. Knowing that homegrown sympathy is the best kind, I decided to spill my guts. With each horrid detail, I milked it for all it was worth. They felt my pain. Mom removed two pieces of perfectly crisp bacon from Dad's plate and placed them on mine. Even better, since Brother Jeff had not yet arisen, she generously gave me his portion as well. Bacon-filled and sympathy-drenched, I enjoyed coming clean. Alas, my joy was short-lived.

After church that Sunday, Dad announced he and I would be walking home together. He told Mom to drive the car while we walked and talked man to man. Instinctively, I knew this was not going to end well for me. Our last father-to-son talk involved why I needed to wear an athletic supporter during Little League baseball games. Through periodic bouts of throat clearing, he explained the reason for my added protection. Too young to fully comprehend the dangers awaiting me but respecting his advice, I wore the apparatus with as much dignity as possible. I was substantially more dignified after Bill Haynes, my Little League coach, informed me the thing was to be worn *inside* the pants. In the third inning of my first game at second base, a ground ball took a wicked hop, bounced, and slammed me squarely in the you-know-where. I appreciated the support.

Mom drove slowly by us as we were passing Andy Stayrook's Auto Sales. Her smile from the car's window looked forced and that put me even more on guard. Dad's small talk chatter should have been the real clue he was building up to something big. He would use the same technique again a couple of years later when our star football player and his cheerleader girlfriend discovered she was with child, a scandalous mishap in small towns like DeGraff. Soon after their news hit the streets, Dad cornered me for our first "birds and bees" talk. The poor man stumbled ponderously through the details. I didn't have the courage to tell him I already knew all I needed to know about sex, having heard a far more enjoyable version from the big guys at The Stump, DeGraff's males-only swimming hole.

Just before we reached Mill Street, Dad dropped a bombshell of atomic proportions onto my little world, creating total destruction with one almost-survivor.

"Rickie, you are going to take dance lessons with your mother and me at the Arthur Murray Dance Studio in Bellefontaine. The lessons begin this Wednesday night."

His words reached my ears, traveled into my brain, then sped down to a pair of disbelieving legs that, in anticipation of the catastrophe poised to humiliate them, stopped me dead in my tracks. A panicked mouth spoke for all other body parts.

"What? Why? Dance lessons? Please, no dance lessons! Why would you and Mom do this to me? Please listen. Philip Rohrer, a great dancer and probably the best dancer in our school's history, says no one can teach anyone else how to dance. Philip knows about dancing. Please Dad, don't make me take dance lessons!"

He looked down on me patronizingly, his face a mixture of sympathy, dismay, irritation, and resolve. Sometimes I could successfully sway my father and sometimes I'd fail. This was

71

failure, and from past experiences I knew the end game. I was basically screwed. His next words sealed the deal, nailed the coffin, and ensured no last minute reprieve from the governor.

"Rickie, no arguing."

I didn't say another word the rest of the walk home. Dad talked enough for both of us, a well-rehearsed oration containing some obviously mother-influenced references about the lifelong benefits of learning how to dance. His words were like bees buzzing through my head so that I only heard small bits and pieces of his monologue sting their way into my brain.

"...your best interest..."

"...girls admire...boys...dance..."

"...Mrs. Curl said..."

"...embarrassed for you..."

"...box step, waltz, fox-trot..."

"...Arthur Murray..."

"...Wednesday night..."

"...will appreciate..."

"...my son..."

As soon as we arrived home, I ran up the stairs to my room, slammed the door, and sank into my bed. Even though I buried my head under my pillow, I could still visualize remnants of Dad's mandate marching around the room while waving big red-lettered, "YOU ARE SCREWED" signs. Somehow within this parade of mockery, I fell asleep.

When I awoke, a strange transformation had occurred, and I'd given in to my fate. The dance lessons were going to happen no matter how much I protested. Once I accepted that simple truth, optimism kicked in. If I took the lessons and learned a couple of nifty steps, Prom Swanson just might ask me to be her Sadie Hawkins partner. And I already had my dance acceptance speech memorized.

Watch out, Philip Rohrer. The dance floor won't be big enough for both of us.

Chapter Ten

ARTHUR, KATHRYN, ELOISE, AND ME

Wednesday came quickly, and although I continued to fake resistance to the dance lessons in order to gain additional sympathy and more crisp bacon strips, I actually felt kind of excited for them to begin. I even agreed to watch the latest episode of *The Arthur Murray Party*, hosted by Arthur and Kathryn Murray.

Late on the afternoon of our first lesson and after I'd delivered *The Bellefontaine Examiner* to my seventy-two customers, Carolyn Haynes knocked on our front door. Carolyn was the youngest daughter of Little League coach Bill Haynes, and as a high school student, she was one of the older women I had a crush on. She'd come to babysit Jeff and Kurt.

A year before Kurt was born, she sat for Jeff and me when Mom and Dad went to a fancy restaurant in Lima with Uncle Richard and Aunt Sally. I was in full show-off mode, and Carolyn told my parents I was a snotty, little brat. Her report hurt my feelings, so I was determined to have her witness me on my best big boy behavior. I greeted her at the door decked out in my blue church suit, mom-ironed white shirt, snap-on bow tie, and polished Buster Browns. I was, in my mind, Cary Grant suave.

"Good afternoon, Carolyn. I'm going dancing with Mother and Father in Bellefontaine this evening."

"Yeah, Rickie, I know. Your Dad told me where you'd be in case I need to contact them. If you learn a cool step or two, especially something fast, maybe you can show me."

Her words inspired me more, and just when I thought life couldn't get any better, she winked at me and said I looked cute. I flushed hot cinnamon red from the top of my freshly buzz-cut head down to my Buster Browned feet. I considered feigning a sudden illness to stay behind in her care, but fortunately had just enough adolescent common sense to realize that no lessons meant no future dances with Carolyn. In that moment of delightful infatuation, Carolyn leapfrogged over both Prom Swanson and Mouseketeer Annette Funicello on my penciled list of dream ladies (a list, by the way, that was in a constant state of flux). A few years earlier, Princess Summerfall Winter-spring, Howdy Doody's attractive puppet partner, topped the list. Now as a fifth grader, I was confident my taste in women was maturing. Even matronly Miss Frances of *Ding Dong School*, a memorable one-time infatuation, had dropped several notches below the rest, although she still retained page one status.

Before we got into the car, I made Jeff promise that he and Kurt would behave for Carolyn, explaining how fortunate they were to be watched by her. Unfortunately, Jeff was too young for fantasy list-making and failed to grasp the significance of my request. When we returned from our lesson, I heard Carolyn tell Mom that Jeff was a snotty, little brat.

The twenty-minute drive to Bellefontaine gave me ample time for backseat thinking, and that led me back to a major worry I'd been fretting over.

"The two of you have each other to dance with. Who will I have?"

Mom answered, "Oh, don't worry, honey. I'm certain there will be plenty of single ladies eager to dance with such a handsome young man."

That made sense, so I crossed "dance partner" off my worry list. We guys always keep our lists—fantasy and worry ones—up to date.

"Will you and Dad be partners for all of the lessons?"

"I don't know. We will have to wait and see."

The worry list temporarily depleted, I focused on my shiny shoes, tying and re-tying the laces to perfect tightness. My feet were in for a big night, and I wanted to be certain they were secure in their shoes.

Dad had a big surprise up his sleeve before we went to the studio, one I suspect he hoped would assist in making me feel better about their dance lesson directive. "How about supper at the Dutch Mill before we trip the light fantastic?"

Of all the places to eat in my Logan County world, Dutch Mill was second only to Taylor's Restaurant in DeGraff. Although we didn't eat at the Dutch Mill often enough, my parents and I were consistent in our menu choices: a foot-long hot dog with extra mustard for me, the deep-fried pork tenderloin sandwich for Mom, and for Dad the Dutch Mill treat, a fried shrimp basket loaded with French fries. With fine cuisine laid out before us, we didn't care how out of place we looked dressed in our Sunday best on a Wednesday evening. To prevent the overflowing mustard from staining my clothes, Mom triple-napkined me from neck to trousers, and for once I didn't mind.

The Arthur Murray Dance Studio was located downtown among Bellefontaine's high-rise buildings. Dad knew the address, and we parked right in front on the street. We walked up several flights of wooden steps to the top floor where the studio was located. A short hallway led to a slightly opened door with "ARTHUR MURRAY DANCE STUDIO" stenciled on the frosted glass. Dad opened the door wider and led us in.

A slender, tall, and stately lady welcomed us. She was dressed in an elegant black gown with a double strand of pearls draped around her neck. A happy-to-see-us smile framed perfect teeth shining as brightly as her pearls. She shook Dad's hand and then Mom's before reaching down to me. Trying not to stare but failing, my eyes locked onto the pearls. Except for the necklace Joan Crawford wore on the Roxie Movie Theatre screen, I had never seen one that extravagant. I wondered how something as homely as an oyster could produce such beauty.

"And what is your name?"

"I'm Rickie." I could tell my hand was clammier than a clam, and I wished I'd wiped it on my pants before extending my palm upward. She politely seemed not to notice.

"Well, Rickie, I'm Miss Charlotte, one of the dance instructors."

I was fancifully envisioning Miss Charlotte and me partnering, even though my head barely extended above her waist, when a gentleman in a white dinner jacket with a red carnation peeking out from the buttonhole joined us. Miss Charlotte introduced him.

"Christopher, this is Rickie and his parents, Lewis and Dortha Jean. They are members of our new class. Christopher is my husband and the other instructor."

I tried not to look disappointed and may have succeeded. As Christopher reached out to shake my father's hand, I quickly swiped mine across the back of my pants in anticipation of our shake. Grandpa Jack taught me how to shake hands with a firm grasp. Hand presentable, I reached up to shake his, and he was impressed.

"Young man, that is quite a gentleman's grip." I couldn't wait to tell Grandpa Jack.

As Miss Charlotte was no longer available, I slowly browsed the room for a potential partner. My hopes dipped well below sea level after I completed the third sweep and sighted couples only. With no other singles, I was on my own, the dreaded third-wheel interloper. I hoped Dad was willing to share his wife.

Clapping her hands while asking us to follow her, Miss Charlotte led us toward the back and a cluster of perfectly spaced wooden chairs. The large room was illuminated by a line of globed fixtures attached to what appeared to be a metal-paneled ceiling. Two four-paned windows facing the street provided the only other source of light, but with nighttime closing in, their usefulness was quickly fading. Between the windows rested a squat mahogany cabinet housing a record player and a row of records angled on its single shelf. The area in front of it was ample for dancing, and I felt at ease as I glanced around.

Miss Charlotte interrupted my surveillance. "Christopher and I are delighted to welcome you to this Arthur Murray dance class. We met in Chicago during training to become instructors, and we were married soon after. We had the wonderful honor of being personally taught by Mr. Murray and his wife, Kathryn. Our goal for each new class is to teach you to dance as professionally as the Murrays taught us."

I was impressed. No run of the mill hoofers, these two were Arthur and Kathryn Murray's real deal "offspring."

Miss Charlotte went into detail about Arthur Murray's background and explained that his studio franchise was the second oldest one in US history, behind A&W Root Beer. She also gave us business cards displaying their simple promise: *If you can walk, we can teach you to dance.* Sounded fair enough to me.

As she began to tell us what we could expect each week, the entrance door behind us creaked open. You could tell the person entering was trying to be inconspicuous, but the attempt was futile. The door's hinges needed oil worse than Oz's Tin Man, and the wider the door opened, the louder the creak. We were all gawking backwards like rubber-neckers passing a pileup. Miss Charlotte paused to watch as well.

"I am so sorry to be late. Gracious me, I am never late for anything! I arrive for doctor's appointments twenty minutes early. I thought the studio was at the south end of Main Street, not north. Anyway, by the time I realized my mistake, it was too late and so am I. I should have left the supper dishes in the sink instead of washing them. I am so sorry! Please, go back to whatever you were doing."

She was embarrassed, and I felt sorry for her. With her reddened face and rapidly blinking eyes, it looked like she was about to cry. To top it off, she was old. I had no idea how old, but she was definitely way up there. I knew my share of old ladies, including my grandmothers, our neighbor Elva Young, and some women on my paper route like Mrs. Waite, Miss Lizzie, and good old Fern Burdette. I didn't know their ages either, but this woman had them by at least a decade. She was hesitant to enter and stood perfectly still within the doorframe, a plain yellow dress with white hair neatly pinned into a mashed-potato-looking bun.

Miss Charlotte saved the day. "Dearie, you have not missed a thing, not one thing. I was just talking about our weekly dance schedule. Now, come over here and join us." I didn't look up as she hurried toward us and sat in the empty chair beside me.

Miss Charlotte emphasized that each week the lessons would progress in difficulty, beginning this first week with the easiest dances, the two-step and the box step. Next week we'd learn to dance the foxtrot, followed by the cha-cha, waltz, and on week five, the jitterbug. We'd be ready to tango, the most challenging dance, by our final week. Although the jitterbug, a Philip Rohrer equalizer, was my target, I decided to give the others their due.

I realized my fate before Miss Charlotte finished our orientation. The late-arriving old lady would be my partner! I kept my head tightly anchored and faced forward, eyes rotating slowly toward the plain yellow dress seated beside me. I saw wrinkled ankles attached to wrinkled legs. Wrinkled hands on wrinkled wrists. A wrinkled neck propping up a wrinkled face. My brow involuntarily wrinkled.

Christopher turned on the record player, and he and Miss Charlotte demonstrated the two-step. The dance seemed simple enough to master. They followed with a box step, and that, too, looked easy. Just before inviting us onto the floor, Christopher explained their basic rule for all lessons. We were to keep the same partner each week. He said couples learning to dance would, God willing, be partners for life with no cut-ins allowed. The adults laughed. Then I swear he shot me a *that's a tough break, kid* look before inviting us to join Miss Charlotte and him on the floor.

I turned my head fully to look at my no-cut-ins-allowed partner, and I swear this is also true. She gave me her own *that's a tough break, kid* look, but with a kinder, more sympathetic expression.

"Hello, young man, I am Eloise. May I have this dance?" Her shining, light blue eyes smiled at me.

"Of course you may, Eloise. I'm Rickie."

I inherited a number of positive traits from my mother. The ability to engage in small talk, however, wasn't among them. I couldn't think of one thing to say as we danced, while the other couples chattered away like magpies. My parents were babbling like Dad had just returned on leave from the navy, and they hadn't seen one another for months. What new could be that interesting since supper?

I'm not certain why I was so quiet. Maybe I was too focused on the music and my silent counts of one-two, one-two, one-two. Maybe I was too concerned about stepping on Eloise's fossiled

Rick D. Niece, Ph.D.

feet, afraid they might crumble. Maybe I was too intent on earning compliments as Miss Charlotte and Christopher glided couple to couple dispersing generous words of praise. Or maybe my small-talk capabilities were too miniscule to be found on a microscope slide. I don't know. I do know I was pathetically left-footed as a conversational dance partner. Eloise, God bless her, did not give up.

Eloise: "Do you like school, Rickie?"
Me: "Yeah."
Eloise: "What grade are you in?"
Me: "Fifth."
Eloise: "What is your favorite subject?"
Me: "Reading."
Eloise: "That is wonderful. What do you like to read?"
Me: "Stuff."
Eloise: "Are those two dancers your parents?"
Me: "Yeah."
Eloise: "They seem nice. Are there others in your family?"
Me: "Yeah."
Eloise: "Are you a nasty little boy who hates dancing with an old lady?"

Okay, she didn't ask that, but I'll bet the thought ran through her head. I wasn't trying to be difficult, I really wasn't. I simply had no idea what to say. She finally caught on and for the remaining dances stopped asking questions and instead talked about herself. I felt relieved and actually enjoyed listening. She was sort of interesting.

Her late husband Walter was one of the first insurance salesmen in Logan County, and in time opened his own agency. He was a wonderful husband with an excellent business mind, and when he died two years ago, he left her well-off financially. Although he had insured them fully for any disaster, there was no policy to insure her from loneliness.

They had a son and a daughter. The son and his wife raised her

80

four precious grandchildren in Spokane, Washington, and the now-grown grandchildren were spread throughout the country. She never saw any of them enough. The eldest granddaughter in Maine was pregnant and due in a few months, and Eloise was anxious to be a great-grandmother for the first time. Her childless daughter and son-in-law lived in Indianapolis, and Eloise was grateful they visited frequently.

Until the birth of her son, Eloise had been a nurse at Mary Rutan Hospital in Bellefontaine. She quit being a nurse to raise him and his sister. After her children entered school, she worked part-time for a general practitioner and really enjoyed it and the reduced hours. Now retired, she lived alone. She said she didn't know why she'd decided to take dance lessons, a very daring adventure that was not at all like her. She'd discussed it with her daughter who encouraged her, and here she was.

"And here we are, and I think it's grand," said Eloise with obvious sincerity. As Eloise was praising the grandness of us being there, Miss Charlotte stopped the music.

"We are finished for this first week. What a marvelous class! Next week we foxtrot."

I said goodnight to Eloise, and she smiled again. "Promise me, Rickie, you will be back for lesson two, right?" I think she was afraid I'd skip out on her.

"I promise." Her bright eyes sparkled.

Mom and Dad talked the entire ride home as they happily relived their dance enchantment. Neither of them seemed overly interested in my evening, and I couldn't believe my mother wasn't giving me a Perry Mason-like interrogation. As we passed the DeGraff city limits sign, she finally asked. "Did you like your partner? She looks rather elderly."

"Yeah, she's nice. Her name is Eloise, and she's a widow. I like her."

"Good, that's good. Your father and I are proud of you. I think we all had fun."

Rick D. Niece, Ph.D.

Just before getting into bed, I practiced the two-step and box step by myself, humming the music softly. I had made a little progress as a dancer, although certainly not yet in Philip Rohrer's league. But I had him in my sights. I was kind of proud of me, too.

Chapter Eleven

WALTER AND BERNIE

All week I pondered potential topics for small talk in anticipation of the next dance lesson and conversations with Eloise. I even scribbled out a two-page list before narrowing the possibilities down to six really good ideas:

- Ned Heintz and his family's farm.
- Our dog, Lady, and how she followed me around on the newspaper route.
- Why Virginia Hittepole's nickname was Skinner.
- My winning shot in the fifth versus sixth grade basketball game.
- Fishing in the Bokenghelas Creek below our house.
- My two bouts with double pneumonia (a really, really good one since Eloise had been a nurse).

I thought about asking Mom for advice, but then decided I was better off on my own with this small talk dilemma. She'd make too big a deal out of it. By the time we got into the car for the drive to Bellefontaine, I was primed to talk. I hadn't spoken much about the first dance lesson except briefly in the car that evening and when we watched the weekly episode of *The Arthur Murray Party*, so I decided I'd be wise to practice my conversational technique while we drove. A bit of warm-up couldn't hurt.

I started by stressing how impressed I was with Miss Charlotte and Christopher, and then I shifted to an Eloise description, worked in her children and grandchildren, and closed with Walter. Dad thought he might have met Walter during a barbershop quartet festival held in Bellefontaine. My smooth and seamless chatter carried us all the way to the studio. Yep, I was Rickie, the small-talk machine.

But during our walk up the steps I panicked, then decided I should share my carefully chosen topics with Mom before I used them on Eloise. Mom was, after all, the family expert. I eagerly watched her face for a reaction. She frowned and asked if I was certain Eloise would find my choices interesting. I assured her I had no doubt. She tilted her head slightly, winked at Dad, and wished me luck. I knew that head tilt and wink. They were definitely not confidence builders, but I vowed to remain confident anyway.

As soon as we entered the studio door, I saw that Eloise was already inside and saving me a seat.

"I arrived early this time," she said with a smile. "I even beat Charlotte and Christopher, and the door was still locked." She was proud of her promptness and repeated the story to each arriving couple.

Miss Charlotte wore a different but equally swanky gown, the string of pearls again gracing her neck. She was, in my mother's words, Loretta Young sophisticated. For this week's lesson, Christopher had on a black tuxedo with a white carnation. The two of them could have been figurines atop a giant wedding cake. They looked that classy. I visualized Eloise and me standing on the cake beside them and giggled out loud at the image.

Christopher described the foxtrot before he and his wife demonstrated the steps. They did it without music, with Christopher calling out the rhythmic beat while their fluid feet followed. Satisfied we knew the basics, they invited us to join them. Just before Christopher turned on the music, Mom came over to give me a quick hug, but I couldn't tell if her hug was one of encouragement or consolation. I cleared my throat for conversation readiness as Eloise and I walked onto the floor. As we began to dance, I led with topic one.

"My best friend Ned Heintz lives on a farm, and they have a herd of milk cows."

"That is nice, Rickie."

Silence

"We have a dog named Lady, and she's part Dalmatian and part Greyhound. She follows me on my paper route."

"Walter and I preferred cats."

Silence

"My best female friend is Virginia, and one time Lady attacked her poodle skirt and ripped the poodle to shreds. Virginia threatened to skin Lady alive, so I nicknamed her 'the Skinner' and it stuck. Everyone in our class calls her Skinner."

"Does she really appreciate being called Skinner? Virginia is such a pretty name. My grandmother's name was Virginia."

Silence

Holy cow, we were just beginning the foxtrot, and I was halfway through the list. This wasn't going at all the way I'd planned.

"A couple of weeks ago I made the winning shot against the sixth grade team in a really rough basketball game."

"Our son played football."

Longer silence

Somehow, we'd made it through the third dance and stayed on the floor waiting for Christopher to change records. Sensing the need for a change of strategy, I turned my next conversational topic into a question.

"Eloise, do you like to fish? We have a creek below our house, the Bokenghelas, and Steve Houchin and I fish there for carp and suckers."

"After Walter died, I lost interest in fishing."

Longest silence

Last topic! Criminy, if Eloise didn't enjoy pneumonia, I was in deep trouble.

"I got double pneumonia two times in the first grade. I almost died twice."

"Walter *did* die from pneumonia."

Dead silence

Well, Walter and I had something in common—I was pretty much a goner, too. What went wrong? Was my life that boring?

When the music stopped the next time, Miss Charlotte asked us all to sit. She and Christopher danced a variation on the foxtrot the two of them had developed, and I acted like I was watching. But my brain was nervously scanning through its meager storage unit of memory in a desperate search for new topics. Vacant, empty, kaput! I was down to zilch.

As the other couples drifted back onto the floor to practice the new steps, Mom motioned me over to her. She leaned down and whispered, "How is it going? Is Eloise interested in your topics?"

"Going great," I lied. "Couldn't be better."

I felt no assurance from her reassuring pat on my head. Eloise remained seated, and I walked back to sit beside her. Not looking at me, she spoke quietly as she placed her hand on my forearm.

"Rickie, can we sit this one out?"

"Sure, no problem, fine with me."

I watched my parents dance the new sequence steps with confidence. I shot them a thumbs up. They were pleased I noticed.

Eloise squeezed my forearm, started to speak, and stopped herself. She tried again, paused, but still said nothing. We were both at a loss for words until she finally broke the silence.

"I am sorry to be so quiet tonight." Another pause. "I just feel sad, and I have felt this way all week."

She kept her hand on my arm. "I have thought more about Walter the past few days than I have in months. I think these lessons tugged at something deep inside of me." She squeezed my arm harder. "I miss him very much."

I didn't know what to say, so I simply placed my hand on her hand resting on my arm.

"Walter and I never danced. He was not able to." She took several long, slow, deep breaths. "Walter had polio." She gripped my arm even more tightly, and feeling awkward, I removed my hand. "He was afflicted terribly in both legs when he was a teenager. He wore heavy braces, and the brace on his left leg was bigger and heavier because that leg had the greater damage. He wore braces his entire life. He learned to walk again after intensive therapy and with the use of crutches, but walking was very difficult and became increasingly harder as he got older." She lowered her head while inhaling a long, slow breath.

"The last ten years were the worst, and he finally agreed to use a wheelchair. The chair embarrassed him. You men are so stubborn, so darned independent. Toward the end, he had pretty much given up, and I had to push him room to room. I hated seeing him so discouraged. When you love someone like I loved Walter, you do all you can. I simply wanted him to be comfortable. He got weaker, became bedridden, and pneumonia finally got the better of him."

She sniffed and took her hand away. I couldn't stand seeing how unhappy she looked, so I stared out toward the floor and my parents. Watching them hold one another, I couldn't imagine Mom without Dad.

"I am very sorry, Rickie, I don't know why I'm burdening you with this. I'm just a silly old bother. I know it's true, and I know it's what my children think. I'm sorry."

For the first time with Eloise, I finally had the right words. I knew exactly what to say. "My friend Bernie is in a wheelchair. He has been in that chair his whole life."

"Bernie? Who is Bernie?"

At that moment we connected with something real, something we both cared about. Goodbye to artificial topics and silly small talk. Hello, Walter and Bernie.

Even though I told Eloise a little about Bernie, his cerebral palsy, and our friendship, the night was Walter's. For the rest of the evening, through every dance and break, Eloise talked about Walter. I think she wanted me to know everything there was to know about him. I was happy to listen because we had four more lessons for me to tell her everything about Bernie.

Eloise and Walter met during his physical therapy sessions at Mary Rutan Hospital where she was a nurse. He was positive his legs would heal, that he would walk again, and life would be normal. Eloise admired his courage and optimism, but as a nurse she understood the devastating effects of polio and the permanent damage the disease had done to his legs. She was upset at Walter's doctor for not being more honest and for filling him with false hope.

"Hope is a good thing, a wonderful thing," said Eloise softly, "but false hope is bad medicine. Oh well, what does a nurse know compared to the all-knowing doctor?"

Initially, they agreed their friendship should be a professional one, nurse to patient. In time, neither was pleased with that arrangement, and after months of formality, they gave in to their mutual attraction and agreed to see one another socially. Their first date was at the Holland Movie Theatre in downtown Bellefontaine for a Bette Davis film. They courted, romance blossomed, and finally, "after what seemed like an eternity," Walter asked Eloise's father for permission to marry her.

"He asked my father before he asked me. Can you believe it! My Walter was old-fashioned that way. Even though Daddy had concerns about Walter's condition, he gave us his blessing. You see, Daddy genuinely respected him. He said Walter had gumption. With his constant struggle to walk wearing those heavy braces and using crutches, Walter sold insurance policies door to door all through Logan County. Daddy admired that."

Eloise agreed that they would honeymoon in Hot Springs, Arkansas, because Walter had heard President Roosevelt went there for therapy on his legs. The hot springs and their steaming, therapeutic waters supposedly had healing powers. The two weeks in Hot Springs convinced Walter that his legs were stronger. Eloise didn't contradict him, but she could not detect any physical proof of improvement. They never returned to Hot Springs.

Suddenly, Miss Charlotte announced the foxtrot dance lesson was over.

"Rickie, thank you for letting me talk on and on about Walter. I feel better. I guess you were my hot springs therapy tonight. See you next week." She kissed me on the cheek, a sweet gesture not unnoticed by my mother.

As soon as Dad started the car and pulled away, Mom began her interrogation. "You and Eloise seemed unusually talkative this evening. And she kissed you. My goodness, your list must have worked well. Did you cover all the topics?"

I was overcome by honesty. "No, not really. The list was a bust. She wasn't interested in any of it. But it didn't matter because Eloise ended up talking the entire lesson about her late husband, Walter. I liked hearing about him. He had polio."

Rick D. Niece, Ph.D.

I told them all about Eloise and Walter, and that seemed to keep Mom's curiosity satisfied for much of the drive. I knew she'd heard all she wanted to know when she yawned and laid her head on Dad's shoulder. She slept the remainder of the trip and didn't awaken until I got out of the back seat to open the garage door.

The next week's lesson was the cha-cha, and before we had cha'ed our first cha, Eloise asked about Bernie. She said she had waited all week to hear about him. That was ironic because I had struggled all week with how to describe the amazing Bernie Jones to her. I decided to start at the beginning, and for the rest of the evening, I was the talker.

"Last year, I took over Billy Neal's newspaper route delivering *The Bellefontaine Examiner.* Dad is certain that peddling newspapers around DeGraff will teach me responsibility and how to manage money better. He's convinced that I squander the twenty-five cents allowance he gives me each week." Eloise laughed, but I wasn't trying to be funny. That's the reason he gave me.

"I have seventy-two customers on my route and like them all, but Bernie Jones is my favorite. His very severe cerebral palsy confines him to a wheelchair because he has no control over any part of his body, except for his eyes. His arms and legs flail around like a wounded turkey. Bernie spends most days, almost all day, parked in his parents' small side yard. Our first meeting was terrible, and I could barely understand a word he said. I have to admit I was afraid to see him the next day when I delivered the paper. Luckily, during our second meeting, I discovered we both like Dick Tracy. Each day when I deliver his paper, I read the *Dick Tracy* comic strip to him and then tell him about my day in school. Bernie can't attend school, but he is really smart. He's funny, too, and..."

90

I went on and on explaining what great friends we were, and how I hoped one day to wheel him out of his side yard and take him around DeGraff. I was still yammering away when Miss Charlotte announced the cha-cha lesson was over. I had monopolized the evening, but Eloise didn't seem to mind.

"Bernie sounds like a great friend, and you are so good to him. When you deliver Bernie's paper tomorrow, be certain to say hello for me. And tell him about my Walter."

I didn't tell her I had already told Bernie everything about Walter and her.

As we hugged good night, she grinned, "I remembered something funny I want to share with you. You will laugh at me. Remind me next week."

I forgot to remind her, and I never heard the story. I'll bet it was a good one.

The waltz and jitterbug weeks danced by quickly, and our conversations continued to flow smoothly. I told Bernie stories, and Eloise shared Walter memories. We were eager talkers and unselfish listeners, a rare and worthy combination.

I liked the waltz, but had doubts it would be a dance of choice at our next school mixer. Eloise really enjoyed waltzing and said it was her favorite. She called it the dance of royalty.

The jitterbug, the focus for our fifth lesson, was my favorite, and I stayed extra alert for the instructions. During one of the breaks, I asked Christopher to teach me a few of his best fast-dance steps, emphasizing I had some young ladies back home to impress. He pulled me aside for a personal tutorial, and I quickly mastered the basic moves as well as a couple of fancy ones he showed only to me.

I tried to jitterbug with Eloise, but she struggled the whole time. Valiant in spirit but slow in body, she couldn't keep

91

pace with feet-flying, hip-gyrating Rickie. I was a dancing terror. Everyone applauded when I ended a singular set with a show-off flourish, even Eloise who was limp in her chair from exhaustion.

After the lesson, I walked her down the long flight of stairs and held her arm in case her legs gave out. Mom said I was the perfect little gentleman.

I dreaded the thought of the next class being our final one, and Wednesday came around too quickly. The whole class was unusually quiet while Miss Charlotte and Christopher described the tango before flawlessly demonstrating its intricate steps. On our first night of lessons, they had warned us about the tango's difficulty, and oh my gosh, the two of them were right. We tried vainly to master the rhythms and capture the dance's braggish attitude, but the tango's spicy South American flavor was well beyond the bland taste of this group of west central Ohioans. Miss Charlotte and Christopher did their best to lead us, switching back and forth among couples while shouting out instructions, but we were a sorry troupe of terrible tangoers.

A few minutes before our usual ending time, Christopher mercifully stopped the music, and our six weeks of lessons were over. Sadness crept in among us. Miss Charlotte and Christopher looked as sad as the rest of us, even though a new class would begin for them the following week. Christopher announced that he and Miss Charlotte had started a tradition several years ago, one in which the couples shared a final dance in celebration of their class's success.

No one was anxious for the last dance. Eloise suggested a waltz, and Christopher chose "The Blue Danube" by Johann Strauss II, the "Waltz King." One by one, each couple, led by my mother and father, walked onto the floor. Eloise and I were last. We did not speak until the closing measures.

"Thank you, Rickie, thank you for putting up with this old lady. I know I was not what you had in mind when you signed up for lessons."

I wanted to say something back to her, something to express how much all of this meant to me. All I could manage was, "I'm sorry I never met Walter."

"Well, my friend, next to Walter, you are my favorite guy." We hugged and promised to keep in touch.

Mom and Dad and I didn't talk on our trip back to DeGraff. The drive was long and empty, almost as much as the following danceless Wednesday evening. We stopped watching *The Arthur Murray Party* for several weeks.

Chapter Twelve
PHILIP REDUX

I was a patient little guy. I don't know the source for my patience, whether developed or inherited, but I've always enjoyed its benefits. Neither Mom nor Dad was particularly patient, so I guess they could be ruled out of any nature/nurture debate. Granddad Niece, the man who patiently built his small mom-and-pop clothing store into a large financial success, was the only other patient member from either side of the family. I never actually heard him quoted on the topic, but if a reporter from *The Bellefontaine Examiner* asked Grandfather to reveal his secret for success, I believe he'd have answered with one word: patience.

I could fish for hours in the Bokenghelas Creek below our house and not get a nibble, yet would continue to wait patiently in hopeful anticipation. Steve Houchin would last about an hour, and Dad not even that long.

During the first year of my newspaper route, I patiently squir-relled away pennies and nickels to purchase General Electric's most modern transistor radio from the Montgomery Ward catalogue. Although the plastic marvel cost thirty dollars plus shipping, a steep price for this low-income paperboy, it was a dandy. WJR in Detroit broadcast my beloved Detroit Tigers baseball games. The radio captured their signal waves and transmitted them into an earpiece snuggled in my left ear. The radio was my electronic highway to Tiger Town.

Thus, as a patient little guy, I tolerated the long months until the next fifth and sixth grade mixer by practicing in the privacy of my bedroom. I'd exhibit my burgeoning talents by dancing with Mom in front of the television when the weekly episode of *The Arthur Murray Party* included a jitterbug. She and Dad generously complimented me for my dancing deftness. Mom and I were great partners, and I was sorry Miss Charlotte and Christopher couldn't critique us.

One glorious day I was able to dance with Carolyn Haynes, who was still high on my dreamgirl list. She had come to our house to babysit Kurt while the rest of us traveled to the Robert Hall store in Dayton for school clothes. Carolyn arrived at the door with an armful of 45s to play on Dad's Silvertone Tru-Phonic Phonograph. I spotted Chuck Berry's "Rock and Roll Music," and with an impulse of preteen nerve, I asked her to dance. She accepted, and for three splendiferous minutes, I experienced my first glimpse of heaven. My heart was the only thing racing faster and soaring higher than my legs, and it almost burst when she bragged we were ready for Dick Clark's *American Bandstand.* As terrific as that sounded, I had an even loftier goal: to be ready for Philip Rohrer.

On the evening of the fifth and sixth grade dance, I saturated my short hair with Dad's Vitalis Tonic, splashed on liberal amounts of Uncle Bob's Old Spice, brushed my teeth twice, and gargled with Mom's mouthwash. I looked sharp and smelled yummy. To be certain I didn't scuff my shoes, Mom volunteered to drive me to the dance. At least that's what she used for an excuse. I think her real reason was to offer me some last minute advice. "Imagine you are dancing with me in our living room. Focus on being confident." Heck, I was so filled with confidence, I felt almost five feet tall.

The dance setup was the same as the year before, except now I was a top-dog sixth grader. Before I sat down, I looked across the room to watch the hapless fifth grade squirts squirming in their seats. They didn't have a clue about what to expect.

Mrs. Ruth Wammes, the new sixth grade teacher, barked out Mr. Bailey's orders from last year. I figured sacred command-ments of that nature were securely archived in the school safe to be entrusted to the next generation of incoming teachers. She finished, and the music began. Little Richard's first wailed notes of his top-of-the-charts hit, "Tutti Frutti," set this little Rickie into motion.

I leapt to my feet and sped down the row with Philip Rohrer trailing closely behind. I grabbed Susie Koogler's hand and pulled a startled Susie to center floor, leaving Philip in the dust with his too-late arm stretched out toward an empty chair. Yep, I was dancin' with a gal named Sue and knew just what to do. We were in perfect beat, perfect melody, perfect harmony. We were now the couple in perfect everything. No one else ventured onto the floor, not Philip Rohrer, not Paul Whitehead, not anyone. The moment was ours.

After Little Richard's last "*lop bam boom*," Susie and I stood motionless. I thought there might be some applause or at least a few cheers, but no one reacted. It looked to me like the bewil-dered fifth graders were still trying to figure out how to snatch some extra cookies and swigs of punch. Honestly, I did not care. They could devour every cookie, chug all the punch, and still not feel as full as I did. I was bursting!

I walked Susie back to her seat and thanked her for the dance. Philip intercepted me before I got to my chair.

"Rickie, when did you learn to dance like that?"

I placed my hands on his shoulders, looked him square in the eyes, and said, "Man, you don't learn how to dance. You feel the music running through your body and move to it."

Okay, that's not what I said. But I think Arthur Murray and Miss Charlotte would have approved if I had. I know Eloise would.

I never saw Eloise again. I guess some promises are not meant to be kept. Funny how someone can have such an impact on you, and you don't even know her last name.

One of my newspaper customers, Mrs. Mary Waite, requested I read *The Bellefontaine Examiner* obituaries to her. While I didn't mind reading them, I did dread the thought that I'd see the name Eloise and wonder if she was my Eloise. Thankfully, in all the years of reading obituaries to Mrs. Waite, not one Eloise was ever listed. I found comfort in that.

In a way, I'm glad I never saw Eloise again. The memory of someone special, and reliving the memory over and over, is usually better than seeing the person and trying to recapture your magical time together. Memories are best when left to live on their own. I am also uncertain what more we might have talked about. We shared so much in such a brief time, and our friendship did not deserve to revert back to insignificant small talk or silence.

Take care of her, Walter. I imagine the two of you are now dancing among the stars.

Fred

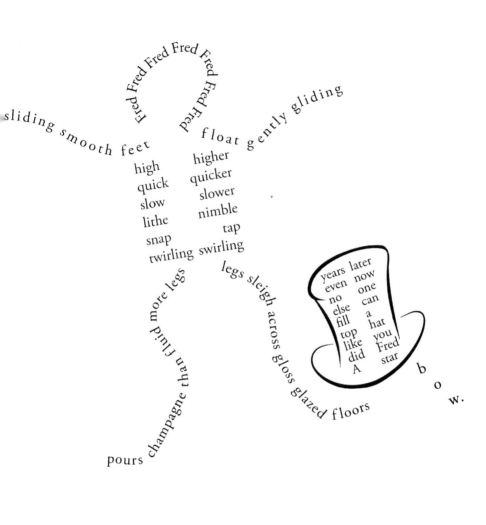

Fred Fred Fred Fred Fred Fred Fred

sliding smooth feet   float gently gliding

high   higher
quick   quicker
slow   slower
lithe   nimble
snap   tap
twirling swirling

legs sleigh across gloss glazed floors

more legs

pours champagne than fluid

years later
even now
no one
else can
fill a
top hat
like you
did Fred
A star

b o w.

PART III

Chapter Thirteen

LEWIS HOBART AND DORTHA JEAN

Saturday, December 6th

"Calling Dr. Kildare…calling Dr. Kildare. Please report to the emergency room."

That was odd. Why were they calling for Dr. Kildare, and which one did they want? Was it Dr. Kildare of the black-and-white movie series starring Lew Ayres in the title role, or television's *Dr. Kildare* played by Sherée's heartthrob, Richard *The Thorn Birds* Chamberlain? Why weren't they also asking for Dr. Gillespie, his medical mentor? I sat up and rubbed my eyes until I was fully awake. Alert now, I listened more carefully as the announcement echoed down again from the waiting room speaker.

"Calling Dr. Sinclair. Dr. Sinclair, please report to emergency."

The stiffness at the back of my neck was an annoying reminder I had not spent the night in our commodious bed at home with my two sorely missed pillows. Glancing around the room, I remembered where I was and why.

As I routinely do when encountering a strange environment, I began taking inventory. I was badly in need of a toothbrush, deodorant, and razor, having not thought to get them from our luggage before Sherée left for Kurt's. I wasn't hungry, but could use a strong cup of hot black tea. I seriously doubted, however, that the hospital cafeteria offered my favored Irish Breakfast morning starter. I ran my fingers through my disheveled hair, hoping not to be embarrassed throughout the day by an unruly mop of bedhead. I quickly chastised myself for shameful self-centeredness. I was focused on personal appearance while surrounded by patients in far worse shape than I. New rule: while visiting a hospital, check vanity at the front desk.

On a positive note, Mom must have gotten through the night, or else a nurse would have notified me. I carefully folded the blanket—a mother-induced gesture of good housekeeping— into a respectable square, rested the pillow on top, and headed for the nurses' station. As I was offering the neatly stacked bedding to one of the on-duty nurses, I started to tell her that I was the son of the lady in Room 424. She didn't look up to acknowledge me. She just scooped up the bundle and nonchalantly pitched it in the direction of a distant laundry cart. She was obviously more focused on the mug of coffee beside her computer keyboard than on me. I watched her for a moment to allow sufficient time for polite atonement. Sensing none was coming, I uttered a sarcastic, "And good morning to you, too." Explicit retributions are the best kind. I strode away with as much dignity as an unshaven visitor who slept in his clothes all night and needed a shower could muster.

Instead of walking directly to Mom's room, I detoured to the men's restroom where I splashed water on my face. The man looking back at me from the streaked mirror over the sink assured us both we were about as presentable as we were going to be for the rest of the day.

When I entered Mom's room, I was surprised to see Dad already sitting there beside the bed holding her hand. I peeked at my watch to verify it was not yet 7:00 a.m. They were so engrossed in one another they hadn't noticed me, so I intruded with a question.

"My gosh, Dad, when did you get here?"

"Oh, I don't know. What time was it, Dortha Jean, a little before six do you think?"

She nodded yes, but I could tell she had no idea of the current time, let alone his time of arrival. By design, I suppose, hospital rooms force patients to be atemporal.

Although he didn't need to, Dad began to justify his reason for coming so early. "Son, you know I can't sleep without your mother beside me. I was awake most of the night before deciding this is where I should be. Neither of us should ever be alone."

He placed his other hand around the hand he was already holding. "She looks better this morning, don't you think?" She did not look better and appeared to be frailer than last night. I avoided answering his question.

"Mom, did you sleep well?"

"I did, I really did. Maybe a night away from your father's snoring helped!" She winked at me and then at him. "That and the fact none of the nurses came in to awaken me to be certain I was sleeping." Dad and I laughed at her joke.

"Rick, sit down. Your father and I were talking about the first time we met and our courtship."

I pulled the room's other chair closer to the bed and sat down. Although I'd heard this story many times before, I wanted to hear it again. Especially now. Their early years took on new importance at that moment, and I felt the need to preserve each detail as intimately as they did.

"Start from the beginning, Lewis, start with when we met at the church." Dortha Jean, the love of his life, was eager to remember. "From the very beginning, for Rick and for me."

Dad floated back in time, and Mom and I journeyed with him.

"I first saw Dodie during a youth group meeting in the United Brethren Church," said Dad. "On that warm evening, late in the summer of 1940, my life began. To be honest, we didn't speak the first night. I was too nervous to say anything, but we certainly noticed one another."

Mom smiled at him and nodded an affirming yes.

"A couple months before, soon after graduating from Lakeview High School, I demolished my father's car in an accident. Since I was at fault, I promised to buy him another one, and it cost all the money I'd saved for college. Ohio Northern had accepted me as a music major, and I was devastated at the setback. To replenish my college fund, I gave piano lessons on Mother's piano and assisted the music teacher at the high school." He reached over to retake her hand, then continued.

"Dortha Jean's mother died in 1939, and her father, your Grandpa Jack, promised she could stay in Huntington to finish school. He promised her, but he didn't keep his promise. Jack, as you know, deserted his family, and his daughter and her younger brothers were on their own. Your mother was in charge and she did her best, but the situation was impossible. Grandma Houchin stepped in and moved the three of them to Lakeview. What an abrupt change for them to live on a farm a mile outside of town, with no running water, no close neighbors, and a single-hole outhouse. Dode's life was turned upside down. But Grandma Houchin, bless her soul, loved her and her brothers. That gracious lady did all she could to make them feel part of a family again."

Mom stretched herself straighter, then lifted her head and

shoulders above the pillow as she prepared herself to add something important to the story.

"Grandma Houchin tried to take the place of our mother, wanting to fill the empty hole in our lives. She almost did, at least for me. She taught me how to cook, to sew and iron, and to clean a house properly. She showed me how to dress like a lady and to do my hair. Best of all, she told me stories about my mother, her daughter. She missed her, too. Once she even—"

Mom paused and momentarily covered her mouth with her hand. Whatever she was thinking and remembering at that moment remained with her. I couldn't tell if she was out of breath or simply decided not to share the thought. She apologized. "I'm sorry, Lewis. I should not have interrupted. Please go on."

She eased back onto the pillow and closed her eyes, her body again seeming to shrink into the bed. Dad waited a respectable silence before beginning again.

"Dortha Jean was such a cutie, and all the boys in her class flirted with her. That did not please the other girls. They were jealous of the new beauty in town and were mean to her. I wanted to flirt with her also, but because I was no longer a student, in school only to assist the music teacher, I thought flirting would be inappropriate. Besides, I was shy and not very confident. Your mother was much more outgoing than I. In fact, after her first day of school, she asked me to walk her home and carry her books. Can you believe that? Out of all her choices, she asked me, but I wasn't up to it. She asked me again the next day, and this time I agreed." He paused and gently lifted her hand to kiss it.

"During our walk, my mind went blank, and I couldn't think of one thing to say. Finally, when we were almost to the dirt driveway leading up to the farmhouse, your mother flashed that glorious smile she always does when she knows something you do not. She told me she had a secret."

Eyes now open, Mom looked at Dad for approval. "Lew, let me tell this." Dad and I leaned in. Although we both knew what she was about to say, we relished in her eagerness to tell us.

"I told your father the church meeting was not the first time I had seen him. He was shocked, but not nearly as much as he was after my second bombshell." She breathed in hard, forcing down an extra dose of hospital oxygen to help carry her words.

"The first day I was in Lakeview, Grandma Houchin drove around the area to acquaint me with my new surroundings. As we were driving slowly by the only clothing store in town, The Urban Store, I saw the cutest guy standing outside by the front door. Grandma said his name was Lewis and that he was the storeowners' son. Now I have to tell you, even in front of his parents' business in his own hometown, the man looked lost. That didn't matter to me because I liked what I saw." She struggled again for air. But, I swear, her eyes had gained life, and in those brief moments of remembering, she was her vibrant self of a youth long ago.

"I then blurted out, to Grandma Houchin's astonishment as well as my own, 'That's the guy I'm going to marry!' Well, she huffed at me, and our tour ended. We headed straight back to the farm."

She eased back again, and Dad bent down to kiss her on the cheek. Watching a seasoned love grown to maturity from first sight is a rare and wondrous thing, and it is particularly wondrous when the lovers are your parents.

"Go on, Lew. I've told my part. You are on your own but don't leave anything out."

Still proud to be her guy, Dad picked up where he'd left off. "Well, needless to say, our romance officially began, and she was mine no matter how many boys flirted with her. But the courtship was a long one with marriage still several years away. World War II barged in, and after the bombing of Pearl Harbor, I decided to join the navy. The day I left for boot camp in Great

Lakes was one of the worst days of my life. Leaving Dodie was hard enough, but equally difficult was seeing my father cry for the first time in my life. He was not a man to show emotion easily." Dad stopped for a moment to sip at the water in Mom's glass.

"I trained to be a signalman, using flags and Morse Code to communicate ship to ship. I was one of twelve from a class of 200 to be promoted to third class petty officer. As a signalman, I was assigned to the George Leonard, a merchant ship, and we transported weapons and supplies to a number of ports. In Naples, I bought Dodie a cameo brooch, and the thought of pinning it on her lifted me through many harrowing days at sea." He looked at her, and I had the feeling he was reliving the exact moment he pinned on the brooch.

"While I was serving, she moved to Lima to work for *The Lima News*. We kept in touch as much as possible through letters and infrequent telephone calls, but the war years were not easy ones for us."

Mom nodded, then spoke. "Rick, they were terrible years, a time in my life I do not like to remember."

We all sat quietly for a moment. I think Dad was uncertain if he should continue or not.

"Go on, Lew, please," Mom implored.

"In November of 1944, after porting in New York City for shore leave, our crew was given two extra days to change ships. As you well know, I am not the spontaneous type and seldom do anything rash."

"Yes, Lewis," she interjected. "We are aware of that. Right, Rick?"

"You are correct, Mom. He is a man of predictable routine."

"I will give you both that, but thank God for once in my life I was both spontaneous and rash. I telephoned your mother and proposed. I told her if she wanted to marry me, she had better get to New York City right away."

This was one of my favorite parts of their courtship story. "Yes," I interrupted, "thank goodness for Uncle Richard's generosity."

"You're right about that, Rick," Dad said before continuing. "Richard got a quick loan on his car and bought his sister a train ticket to Grand Central Station. I convinced our navy chaplain this romance was more than a one-night stand—hasty marriages were a wartime folly—and he waived the mandatory three-day waiting period for blood tests. On a cold, drizzly November 29th, this amazing lady with a broken garter belt and stringy wet hair became my wife. The rain did manage to keep her orchid corsage and my rose boutonniere fresh, flowers given to us by my captain and our only wedding gift. And as you know, Rick, your mother and I celebrated anniversary number fifty-nine last week." He paused and leaned over to kiss her cheek again.

"A few months later, I received an honorable discharge, and soon after was accepted into the Oberlin College Conservatory of Music with the GI Bill allowing us to afford the tuition. During our first year in Oberlin, you were born, and the best years of our lives waited before us."

He eased back into the chair, as satisfied with his telling of their story as he was with the story itself. But this time, he was not finished. Turning to look at me, he made the strangest request. "Son, take off your shoes and socks and lift your feet to me."

I was puzzled and thought he was joking. His expression, fatherly resolute and retrospective, revealed he was not. I obediently removed my shoes and socks, then raised my feet toward him without question. He cradled them in his hands.

"Dodie, do you remember what I asked the first night we brought Rickie home from the hospital, when he was in his bassinet, and I reached down to hold his bare feet?"

"Of course I remember. You asked, 'Where will these tiny feet take him during his lifetime?' Do you remember what I answered?"

Dad nodded. "You said that his journey, wherever it may lead him, will be a joy for us to follow."

I sat there with my adult feet resting in my aged father's hands, unable to look at him or my mother. At that moment my only thought was that these feet had taken me to the place where endings begin.

Chapter Fourteen
GRANDPARENTS

Amid moments of comfortable silence after snippets of small talk, I sensed my parents wanted to be by themselves. I ventured down to the second-floor cafeteria for a cup of hot tea and wheat toast, claiming a small table in the warmly lit quiet of a back corner where I could eat my breakfast in relative privacy. The courtship story, with its tiny traveling feet conclusion, had left me feeling melancholy and craving a Greta Garbo-like moment: I wanted to be alone. The overdone toast and lukewarm tea didn't help my mood.

I thought about Grandma Houchin, the legendary woman I never met. As a matter of fact, I had seen only one picture of her, a black-and-white photograph Uncle Richard keeps in their family album. In this photo, she and husband Frank are surrounded by their eleven children, and no one is smiling—the usual countenance for photographs from that era. In the picture, Mom's mother, Naomi, is captured forever as a twelve-year-old.

I was grateful for what Grandma Houchin provided my

mother and uncles those many years ago. Who knows how their story might have turned out had she not intervened? She took the three of them under her wing when Mom needed someone to watch over her as she watched over her brothers.

Grandma Houchin died in 1945. After her death, Uncle Ude managed the farm. Mom lamented the farmhouse's decline under his guidance, a condition she swore Grandmother Houchin would have deplored. When I was a kid, I didn't understand her concern. I looked forward to our frequent visits to see Uncle Ude, and admired where he lived and how he lived. Granted, the farmhouse was the messiest, most unkept household imaginable. I guess my admiration was a young boy's dream of never-having-to-clean-your-room dishevelment. The kitchen was a disaster with pots, pans, and dishes filling the sink and countertops, along with an incalculable number of cats.

None of these cats had real names, not even Uncle Ude's favorites. He simply referred to each one as "Kitty." During one of our visits, I decided they deserved names, but quickly understood his reason for feline namelessness. There were simply too many of them. Plus, they all looked alike. Therefore, they collectively remained "Kitty."

Poor Ude was my mother's perpetually repeated example of what happens to a bachelor who does not make his bed daily—he remains forever eligible. In her logic, if you don't make your bed for one day, followed by another day, and then by a series of other days, your will for cleanliness is hopelessly lost and your whole household goes to hell. She sincerely believed that one day of not making your bed led inexorably to domestic Armageddon. With Uncle Ude as the show-and-tell model of undeniable truth, who was I to doubt her? Even now as I visualize him, I see a round and kindly face smiling a single tobacco-stained incisor, a tooth somehow having avoided its companions' fate. Dental hygiene was yet another of his daily negligences.

Years of maintaining the farm on his own eventually took its toll on Uncle Ude, and his health declined. Eventually, he was a slumped-over shadow of agedness. He died in the farmhouse, as had his mother. We attended his funeral, and I remember being disappointed at the small number of people who were there. If not for family, the church would have been empty.

After the funeral, Dad asked Jeff and me to go with him to the old farmhouse. He wanted to see it again, fearing this might be the last time. Mom and my uncles were meeting with an attorney to review the will and determine the property's fate.

Dad drove slowly along the dusty, gravel road leading to the farm. When we parked, I wasn't certain if we were getting out of the car or not. After a moment, Dad asked Jeff and me to follow him onto the porch. He spoke quietly without looking at either of us.

"About a year after your mother and I were married, we spent a pleasant afternoon with Grandma Houchin. That day, for the first time, she admitted she was suspicious of me when Dodie and I started dating. She said it took awhile, but I finally won her over. I was pleased to hear that. She was a tough old bird, but I won her over."

He moved closer to touch the front door. "We were standing on this exact spot, your mother and I, and this door was open while Grandma Houchin told us goodbye. As we walked down the porch steps, she called my name, and I turned to face her. She was an imposing figure framed within the door's shadow, and she spoke with an equally imposing voice. To this day I remember her exact words."

He collected his emotions before continuing. I had never before seen my father this somber. "You take care of my motherless child, Lewis. You take care of her." His eyes welled up, and he dabbed at them with the back of his hand. After a moment, he composed himself. "I promised her I would. You know, those were the last words she ever spoke to me. She died that night." He still had not looked at Jeff or me. Instead, he stared ahead through the closed front door and into the vast universe of emptiness now living behind it.

I admired my father then as I admire him now, a man doing exactly what Grandma Houchin had requested of him with her final words—taking care of her motherless child. He has done so faithfully in sickness and in health, to love and to cherish, till death do them part. I doubt even Grandma Houchin, in the entirety of every bedtime prayer, expected that degree of lifelong commitment from a guy looking lost while standing in front of his parents' clothing store.

Dad's intuition was right. Before he was able to visit the farm again, the homestead was sold and all of the structures, including the farmhouse and barn, were torn down. The siding and wooden beams, it turns out, were more valuable than the buildings themselves. My concern, however, was more pragmatic. I hoped Uncle Ude's beloved litters of Kitty copycats found comfortable lodging elsewhere.

My mother constantly referred to Grandma Houchin as the prime example of a perfect grandmother. Because of this, my grandmothers, Ruth Geyer and Marie Niece, seldom measured up to her impossible standard. Mom could be judgmental with the best of them, a trait I inherited from her and guard against daily. We all have demons to conquer.

Grandma Ruth was Grandpa Jack's third wife. Although she had another family of children and grandchildren in Swayzee, Indiana, she graciously agreed to live in Lima close to his family. After Grandpa Jack's debilitating heart attack from which he never fully recovered, he agreed to move to Swayzee. She wanted to be closer to her family, and he required constant care. The compromise was amicable, and they lived out their lives in comfortable contentment.

I missed them both and greatly anticipated our infrequent but extended visits to their modest, two-bedroom house just outside the city limits sign. Our family of five slept in the single guest bedroom, Kurt in bed with our parents and Jeff and me on the floor in sleeping bags. I enjoyed the pseudo-camping experience with a roof over our heads and the convenience of bathroom facilities just down the hall.

Grandma Ruth made the best fried chicken north or south of the Mason-Dixon Line, her morsels of tastiness putting the Colonel's recipe to shame. Even today, the aroma of chicken frying takes me back to my Grandma's kitchen, crisping pieces of crunchy deliciousness oiling paper towels as they cooled on the countertop. For dessert, her lemon pound cake was delicate, moist, and deep-rich in sponginess. While everyone else enjoyed theirs with strawberries and ice cream, I liked mine unencumbered by conflicting flavors. When I was in college, she'd routinely send me cakes twice a semester. Between her pound cakes and Jinny Knief's molasses cookies, I was one sugar-hyped, happy guy.

She also baked sinfully tempting pecan pies, a devilish temptation for diabetic Grandpa Jack. The man's willpower wilted in the presence of her pecan delicacies. Against everyone's protest, especially my mother's and Grandma Ruth's, he'd cut himself a small sliver and top it with a nickel-sized dab of homemade whipped cream, while promising the little piece was all he wanted. We knew better than to believe him—even Kurt who was barely a squirt—since he had deceived us before.

In the dead of night, he'd sneak into the kitchen for a triple "sliver" topped with silver dollar-sized dollops. The results were always the same. For the rest of the night, he'd be violently ill. But he didn't care, not even during the next morning's inevitable lectures from his wife and daughter. He'd smile at them both and swear pecan pie was worth any distress. I admired his misplaced determination.

Grandma Ruth was also a wonderful seamstress who could sew almost anything to factory-made perfection. Most of my pants, usually purchased from The Urban Store, were too long, and I would closet them until our next Grandma Ruth visit. Once during the zenith of my smart-alecky stage, Grandma was measuring the inseam of my newest pair of dress trousers. She pulled the measuring tape a bit too high on the inside of my upper leg, and in typical sassy-mouthed recklessness, I smirked, "Hey, let's not get too personal." She didn't say a word, but I was shamed by the look she shot me. Sensing I had crossed the line of decency, I quickly delivered my first big boy apology: "I'm sorry, Grandma Ruth, that was not very nice for me to say." Some apologies, no matter how sincere, are not enough. After finishing the measurements, she pinched my cheeks harder and longer than usual. Her thumbprints made quite an impression.

Whereas Grandma Ruth was the stereotypical grandmotherly type in how she looked, cooked, fussed over, and hugged, Grandmother Niece was...well, the best description is stoic. She seldom allowed herself to be caught smiling. I suppose working twelve hours a day, six days a week in The Urban Store sapped the joy out of enjoyment.

She spent her sparse spare time caring for flowers. Her trophy was an African violet that blossomed into an impressive beauty and was proudly displayed on the dining room table. A legendary tale within the Niece family involves that African violet. One evening, after an exceptionally long day of selling clothes, Grandfather Niece poured himself a tall, neat glass of gin before going to the bedroom to change into pajamas. Grandmother Niece filled a similar glass with clear, fresh tap water for her pampered violet. As fate controls these things, she momentarily sat the glass beside her husband's glass before tending to the flower.

When Grandfather returned to sip his drink, he tasted plain water instead of the much-anticipated spirits. Puzzled, he called out to his wife to ask what had happened to the gin. Simultaneously fearing the worst, they rushed together to the violet, an obvious teetotaler now shriveling into a shrinking violet. Death came quickly.

Grandmother shrieked, "Old fool, you've killed my African violet!"

Grandfather shouted, "Old lady, you've wasted a perfectly good glass of gin!"

From that evening on, Grandfather drank amber bourbon, and Grandmother tended the flowers in her garden.

Christmas Day was a mixed blessing for my brothers and me. We'd unwrap our gifts at home in the morning, then drive to Lakeview in the afternoon to celebrate with Dad's family. We were not jubilant about the arrangement, but it was our tradition. As kids, we were permitted to take only one of our presents with us, an always-difficult decision. Until Kurt became wiser, I was able to convince him to select one of mine for his traveling choice.

When I was eight, I received my favorite Christmas gift from my grandparents: a Disney slide projector that illuminated strips of Walt's and my favorite cartoon characters on the wall. For once, I was popular among my older cousins. We flopped on the floor in the large guest bedroom and watched every strip several times. I savored the viewings and my time in the spotlight.

The following year, Grandmother Niece enrolled in a ceramics class, and from that point on we were no longer given fun gifts, only ceramic ones. Each Christmas drive to Lakeview, Jeff and I would mockingly guess what kind of ceramic gift we'd receive. Although Dad scolded us for our ungrateful behavior, I know he commiserated with us.

The mocking turned out to be another miscalculation of my youth. Today our house is decorated with a variety of ceramic gifts from Christmases long ago. I wouldn't trade any one of Grandmother's treasures for a dozen Disney cartoon cels, even if Walt himself signed them. But these many years later, I would trade almost anything else to have Dad's family gather for one more Christmas afternoon at my grandparents' home.

Except for the summer when we painted their house, I didn't experience many private moments with Dad's parents. The older I got, the more I regretted not knowing them better. Finally, a few years before Grandfather Niece died of cancer, I had a chance to be alone with the two of them. I'd gone with my parents to a Niece family reunion at Uncle Robert and Aunt LaVelva's house in Ada, and it was dark by the time all of us began to leave. Neither of my grandparents liked driving at night, so I volunteered to drive them in their car to Lakeview with Mom and Dad following us.

I enjoyed the ease of our conversation and their interest in my career. At the time, I was a high school English teacher and enrolled in a master's program at Kent State University. I shared my goal of one day earning a doctorate and being a college dean. When I finished, my grandfather lamented, almost like a confession, that he and my grandmother had not graduated from high school. He said they were both embarrassed for not setting a better example for their children and grandchildren.

I was dumbfounded. This pair had set an irreproachable example through their family values, work ethic, business success, and community service. We had just left a reunion crowded with their legacy. Even without a formal education, they could each hold their own intellectually with anyone. I knew I'd never attain their cumulative wisdom no matter how many degrees I collected.

I have always been good at expressing myself, but that moment was the first time I prayed for the perfect words. I had to make them realize they hadn't failed any of us. I spoke earnestly and forcefully for the remainder of our drive. I wanted them to be absolved from what they had spent their lifetimes regretting.

From the firm hugs they each gave me at the door, my first real hugs from either, I think they believed me. I hope it lasted.

Chapter Fifteen
BREAKFAST WITH JEFF

Jeff startled me. I was so lost in thought that I hadn't seen him come up to the cafeteria table. My brother is a firm believer in beginning each day with a contractor's heaping helping of a jump-start breakfast, and his overflowing tray was testament to his hearty morning appetite.

"We have a job to finish in Ventana Canyon or the company faces a penalty. I can't stay long but wanted to pop in to see Mom. She and Dad thought you might be down here, so I decided to join you for breakfast."

Spotting my half-eaten toast and cup of cold tea, he chided me. "Is that what you university types refer to as breakfast? Tea and toast? My goodness, man, I'll bet that's the same breakfast your hero, Mr. Chips, nibbled at each morning. Am I correct?"

I didn't have a clever response, and it was probably for the best. I could never top a Jeff putdown, so I changed direction and went for conversation instead. "How do you think Mom looked?"

He shook his head. "She's worse than yesterday. She can't breathe, and she's not eating. Nothing for dinner last night, and her breakfast today was untouched. I can tell that Dad is worried."

He longingly eyed his food but continued talking. "You looked spaced out when I walked up. I stood in front of you for several seconds before you noticed me. Thinking about Mom?"

"I was, but not in a morbid sense. I was thinking about the two of them and their life together. Dad retold the courtship story this morning. My gosh, the two of them have been a couple forever. I must admit I enjoy hearing about their lives before us."

He chuckled while demolishing a strip of crispy bacon, brittle-crunchy just the way I like it. I was getting hungry watching him, but wasn't going to admit it.

"Was it the same story, same sequence?"

"Kind of, but this time he added a new twist at the end. I'll tell you about it later when you have more time."

He simultaneously attacked a pancake stack and a powder-sugared slab of Texas-cut French toast, doubling an impressive hunk of each with his fork. Yes, I was definitely hungry and reached down for the remnant of wheat toast, now thoroughly dried out but still possibly edible.

"Want some of mine?" he offered, motioning toward one of his plates.

"Nah," I answered, "this is fine. I seldom eat breakfast." My stomach rumbled.

As Jeff emptied his plates, I went to the counter to get fresh coffee for him and another hot tea for me. When I returned, I asked the question we'd both been avoiding.

"Do you think she'll make it?"

My tea needed more sugar. But even after adding another pack and stirring it in, the next sip still tasted bitter.

"No, I don't think she will, and I'm afraid Dad won't either. We'll have to take care of him the way he's taken care of her," Jeff answered softly.

We looked at each other then glanced away, neither knowing what to say. After several seconds, Jeff mercifully broke our silence.

"Kurt has a friend, Gary, who is a respiratory therapist and works with preemies here in the hospital. He helps them to breathe until they can manage on their own. Well, the other day Kurt asked Gary to explain to me what's happening to Mom. I made certain that Dad wasn't around to hear his answer. I don't know if I completely understood everything he said, but he's certain she's not going to get better. He told me the formal name of her disease and stressed that at this stage it is almost always fatal. I knew I'd forget what it's called, so I wrote it down."

He fished around in his billfold, pulled out a small slip of folded paper, and handed it to me. Jeff's handwriting is as bad as mine—we both learned cursive from the same teacher who complained to our parents that we were hopeless—and I had to ask him to interpret what he'd written. He didn't have his reading glasses, so his handwriting combined with aging eyesight made the words even more of a struggle.

"That letter is an uncrossed 't' I think, and that one might be a 'u.' Yeah, that's it, the disease is called idiopathic pulmonary fibrosis." I remembered the name from when Mom was first diagnosed. "Gary said it causes her lung tissue, which is composed of little fiber-like fingers, to harden and crystalize. At least that's the way I understand it. As the damage progresses in each lung, the less capacity she has. Eventually there is no capacity at all, and she won't be able to breathe even with supplemental oxygen." He paused to compose himself.

"That's why I asked Kurt to call and let you and Sherée know how serious this is. He's convinced Mom is nearing the end of her battle." He stopped to sip his coffee, but his hand was shaking. Words of distress reveal themselves in different ways. "I guess I agree. I'm glad you're here."

As Jeff steadied his coffee, I watched him breathing easily, deeply, and oh so taken-for-granted naturally. I marveled at the efficiency of breathing when everything works properly breath after breath, hour after hour, day after day. Who even notices?

He put his cup down. "Anyway, that's what's going on. I'm certain the doctor can explain it better."

I tried another taste of bitter tea, then pushed the cup and saucer away. We needed another topic.

"Earlier you asked me what I was thinking about when you came up to the table. To be honest, I was also remembering our grandparents and wishing we'd spent more time with them. I sometimes wonder how they felt about us. Do you think we were good grandchildren?"

Jeff rubbed his forehead, a forehead growing wider and higher into the receding hairline. "I never really thought about it, but yes, of course I was a good grandson. I can't speak for you, big brother. You were always so serious around them." He smiled. "They thought I was funny. I always made them laugh."

"Well then, funny guy, what is your best grandparent memory?"

He answered with no hesitation. "That's an easy one. Remember our home run derby marathon in Swayzee?"

I should have known his answer. Of course his best memory would be anything involving Grandpa Jack. Jeff was Grandpa Jack's favorite.

"Home run derby. Great call, little brother, great call!"

"I thought you'd like it." He looked at my watch. "Holy crap, how did it get to be that late? I've got to run. Give Mom a kiss for me and tell her I'll be back later. In the meantime, I suggest you get yourself some more of that delicious looking toast. You look hungry." As he hurried toward the door, he turned and called back to me, "Goodbye, Mr. Chips." He grinned at his clever allusion.

After I was sure he'd gone, I went to the counter and ordered pancakes, French toast, and a double helping of very crisp bacon. Even Mr. Chips needs nourishment.

Chapter Sixteen
A GOOD THING
TO SAVE

Any day we played home run derby in our front yard was a good day. When Dad had time to join us, it was a great day. We based our game on the television program, *Home Run Derby*, a weekly sports competition between two Major League baseball players. The rules for home run derby are simple. Each batter is allowed three outs per inning, and any hit other than a home run is an out. A swing and a miss, an embarrassing whiff Dad occasionally experienced, is also an out.

The three of us rotated through the minimal positions of batter, pitcher, and outfielder. If the outfielder caught the ball, regardless of how far it was hit, it was an out. The pitcher was supposed to throw easy down-the-middle lobs with no junk. We had to keep a close eye on Jeff because if he was behind in the score, he'd try to sneak in a knuckleball, an unfair disadvantage for the batter.

We couldn't use a real baseball for our front yard games, as the neighbors' windows and ours were too plentiful and vulnerable. So we played with Wiffle balls. That was one of the reasons we enjoyed our not-frequent-enough journeys to visit Grandpa Jack and Grandma Ruth in Swayzee. They had the perfect playing field beside their house: a lush, windowless meadow with an actual fence for us to smack home runs over. The fence made us feel like true big leaguers because a ball hit over it was going, going, gone. With a fence to aim for, there were no disputed calls and no Willie Mays' over-the-shoulder basket-catch theatrics. The fence made our home runs big league real.

Jeff and I wanted to use actual baseballs for home run derby games in the meadow, but Dad insisted on tennis balls. To resolve the dilemma, the three of us met like a baseball commissioner's appointed committee, and after a brief but heated debate, Dad won, and we agreed on tennis balls. Because he was an older guy with slow reflexes, his reasoning had logic behind it. He figured a line-drive tennis ball off his forehead would cause less damage than the thwack of a baseball. His concern was a valid one—Jeff and I had both nailed him in previous games.

To make our games even more like the television program, we each assumed the name of our favorite baseball player. I was always Al Kaline, the future Hall of Fame right fielder who played twenty-two years for the Detroit Tigers. Al was my boyhood hero. Jeff chose Ted Kluszewski, the slugging, sleeveless Cincinnati Reds first baseman. Dad laid claim to being Heinie Manush. At first, Jeff and I thought he was just trying to be funny by using a made-up name. I did some research and found out Heinie Manush was not only an actual baseball player, he'd also been inducted into the Hall of Fame. Dad's Uncle Roy once saw Heinie play at old Navin Field in Detroit.

Our most memorable home run derby game occurred in the meadow, and it was a contest we still consider to be the quintessential fall classic. We began play on a Saturday morning and continued, with breaks for food and darkness, through Sunday. Since we were leaving to return home to DeGraff early Monday morning, we agreed beforehand to play until dusk on Sunday.

We'd been planning the marathon for weeks, and in preparation had brought three mitts, two tennis balls (plus a baseball just in case Commissioner Dad had a change of heart), and a Gene Freese miniature souvenir baseball bat. Jeff bought the bat during a Reds' game at old Crosley Field. Gene Freese was not among his favorite players, but Gene had been traded to Pittsburg and his souvenir bats were half-price. Jeff knew a bargain. The smaller bat was perfect for our game because a regular-sized bat hitting a tennis ball generated too much power. We were all decent hitters, and the smaller bat made hitting a home run more challenging.

Grandpa Jack didn't miss a pitch, an out, or an inning of the marathon. He sat in an ancient lounge chair with his feet propped up on an old tree stump and his favorite Panama straw hat perched on his head. A truly impartial fan, he didn't choose sides, but his lack of partiality didn't deter him from frequent bursts of enthusiastic cheering. As the home runs were plentiful, he was a busy and boisterous one-man fan club.

The incalculable number of knocks during our slugfest eventually took their toll on the Gene Freese "lumberette," and the bat cracked during one of Jeff's Sunday afternoon clouts. Grandpa Jack hurried back to the garage to retrieve a fat roll of sticky black friction tape, the precursor to today's duct tape.

During the remainder of the day, the crack grew bigger and the tape thicker as we continued to add more. Finally, after one of Dad's home runs, the bat had enough and split in half from the handle, through the trademark, and up to Gene's name on the barrelhead. We used the remainder of the tape to mend it one last time, but it was soon beyond repair. The game ended with Gene Freese in two life-support pieces barely bound together by countless strips of now shredded friction tape. We were batless, and the marathon of many innings ended with friendly hugs. Grandpa said we were all winners, and on that most rare of rare occasions, we agreed.

After gathering our gear and walking back to the house, Dad dropped the bat into a garbage can inside the garage. Grandpa Jack retrieved it immediately. "This bat is a happy memory, and a happy memory is a good thing to save." Cradling the remains, he removed his rake from a large nail hammered into a wall stud in the garage and hung the bat in its place.

Each time we visited Swayzee after our historic game, Jeff and I would look in the garage to see if the bat was still hanging in its sacred place of honor. It always was. We liked to imagine Grandpa Jack smiling daily at the bat and reliving his happy memory.

Grandpa Jack died several years later in the back seat of their car. Grandma Ruth and one of her daughters were returning from a shopping trip to Fort Wayne, and he was sitting alone behind Grandma. At one point during the trip, she thought she heard a slight moan, but it wasn't loud enough to cause alarm.

After the funeral and our return to Grandma Ruth's house for a family meal, Jeff and I went outside to look in the garage. We were pleased to see our broken home run derby bat still occupying its place of glory. Out of respect, we left it there on its nailed resting place.

There have been many times since that day I've wished we had taken the bat with us. A happy memory is a good thing to save.

Chapter Seventeen
EMERY BETHEL

After my atypically heavy breakfast, I walked the two flights of stairs to Mom's floor. Exercising instead of using the elevator gave me a sense of caloric burn-off satisfaction, plus the delusion that I was exorcising fat-inducing demons. I can fool myself quite convincingly.

Sherée and Kurt were in the room with Dad. I hugged Sherée, and we shared words of missing one another, albeit an absence of only one night. She then took over as her husband's keeper.

"I brought your toothbrush, toothpaste, deodorant, and hairbrush. I cannot believe I forgot to leave them for you last night."

When she asked if I wanted to go with them to breakfast, and I told her I'd already eaten, she was surprised. After I detailed what I had eaten, her surprise turned to understandable skepticism. "You never eat breakfast!" she exclaimed.

"I know, but Jeff shamed me into it. I think the three of you should go to the cafeteria while I stay here with Mom."

The thought of my breakfast must have whetted their appetites and given Sherée an even better idea. "Boys, let's skip the hospital food and make a run to Denny's. More choices, don't you think?"

I hugged Sherée and whispered, "Try to talk to Dad about what's going on here. See if you and Kurt can team up and get him to understand how serious this is." She assured me she'd do her best.

After they left, I went into the men's room to brush my teeth and freshen up. When I returned to Mom's bedside, her eyes were closed, but I could tell she wasn't asleep. When she opened her eyes, I asked her if she was tired and wanted to sleep.

"Not yet, no. Let's talk for a while. We seldom talk enough. You are always in such a hurry."

Her words stung, but she was right. A career and its pressures too often get in the way of a son's real priorities.

"After we talk, I can rest."

She again closed her eyes and breathed in steady streams of hospital air to fill her lungs as much as possible. I sensed she was trying to take in enough oxygen so that she could sustain a conversation. I reached out to take her hand, an uncommon gesture for me. "Mom, you haven't been eating. The doctor and nurses are concerned, and so is Dad. We are all concerned."

Her eyes shot open, and she pulled her hand away. "I'm not hungry. I'm *not*. I will eat when I am hungry and not before. You, of all people, should know that."

My comment had annoyed her, and she remained silent as the seconds for valued conversation ticked away. I sat scolded. She lay motionless. From past experience, I knew I was wise to remain quiet but felt guilty anyway. If I said something more, it would be taken as an affront. Mothers and sons sometimes find ways of misinterpreting one another.

Then, as though nothing had happened and almost like I'd just arrived, she reached for my hand.

"Emery Bethel died, didn't he?" The essence and suddenness of her question startled me.

"Yes, he did. Why do you ask?"

"I've been thinking about him and Betty and our house on Mill Street. The two of them were such good neighbors, and they were good Christians. Baptist, I believe."

Emery Bethel was the school superintendent and Dad's boss for most of the years we lived in DeGraff. The Bethels lived directly across the street from us, and the close proximity made for several awkward situations. In time, however, Mr. Bethel became a major influence on my life. I decided to be a teacher because of him. He even trusted me to borrow several of his treasured classical music albums. My favorite was Tchaikovsky's "1812 Overture" which featured actual cannon shots instead of a tympani at the conclusion. I first heard the "Overture" on Mr. Bethel's modern high-fidelity record playing system. When he asked me what I thought about it, I was unable to express the magnificence of what I had just experienced.

I was in the eighth grade when rumors of school consolidation hit the streets of DeGraff and Quincy, the small town three miles to the west of us. The next year, the merger was complete. The Great Miami River ran between the two towns, and our shared waterway led to the new school district being named Riverside with a pirate as the mascot. The consolidation was controversial and challenging for everyone involved. Both schools, the pride of their respective communities, were steeped in decades of tradition and alumni pride, and each wanted to retain its unique identity, an impossible outcome.

The choice of a pep song was another flash point. Choosing one school's song over the other was out of the question, so Dad was asked to write a new one. He composed a spirited original and even wrote the lyrics, a creative work that was accepted by all. I'm proud to say it remains Riverside's fight song today.

The residents of Quincy wanted their superintendent to be appointed as Riverside's executive head, but the board of education named Mr. Bethel instead. Even though his selection was upsetting to some, Emery Bethel turned out to be the right man to bring the two schools together. His calm manner, mixed with a firm and confident leadership style, made the difficult transition manageable for both communities. And Mom was correct, he and his wife Betty were good neighbors.

Mom and I both paused for a moment as we each remembered something about the Bethels and DeGraff. I spoke next.

"Betty died first from cancer. After that, I lost track of Mr. Bethel. I've admired very few people as much as I admire him. In my inaugural address, when I became president of the University of the Ozarks, I mentioned Mr. Bethel as being a major influence on my life and career. Do you remember me saying that?"

She nodded a hesitant yes, as she would often do when she really didn't remember something.

"Well, I thought he might enjoy knowing about his impact on me, so I telephoned Jinny Knief, someone who never loses track of anyone, to get his address. She told me he was living in a nursing home outside of Dayton. I wrote Mr. Bethel a long letter and included a copy of my speech and the inaugural program. A few weeks later, I received a reply, but the letter was from one of his nurses. She informed me he was in the late stages of Alzheimer's and had been noncommunicative for more than a year."

Mom winced. "I cannot imagine him like that. Emery Bethel was the most articulate and intelligent man I've ever known. How awful to think of him with Alzheimer's." She turned her face away from me.

"The nurse also mentioned she read him my letter twice and placed it and the program, propped open to a page with my picture on it, on his nightstand. She said he didn't respond, and I guess to make me feel better, she emphasized that he seldom responded to anything. She promised to keep me informed about him, but I didn't hear from her again. The following year Jinny Knief mailed me a copy of *The Bellefontaine Examiner* containing his obituary."

She turned back to me, sat up a little straighter in bed, and touched her hand to her mouth. "My goodness, I have not thought about that for years." More extended breaths. "Not in years. Oh my goodness!"

"What, Mom, what haven't you thought about in years?"

"The time Mr. Bethel and I had our dust-up. I was so angry with him. And, Rick, it was about you and a boy from Quincy. I can't remember his name. The two of you had a fight in school."

Wow, she was going way back. "Mom, it wasn't a fight." I needed to qualify my defensive response. "Well, I guess it looked like one to the teacher, but it wasn't a real fight. We were just goofing around like boys do."

Even now, these decades later, she wasn't buying it.

"Whatever you want to call it, fight or not, Mr. Bethel punished you and that boy."

I chuckled. "Yes, he did. That boy was Jim Cox, and you are correct, he was from Quincy. Mr. Bethel did discipline us, but it was classic Bethel, actually more of a humiliation than a punishment. He was disappointed in both of us, but probably more so with me."

I looked at Mom and could tell she was getting tired. Her exhaustion, however, was not going to interfere. She had more to say, more she wanted to tell me, and the nap could wait.

"As I remember it, his punishment and what he made the two of you do started out fair and appropriate, but your father and I thought it went on too long, that Mr. Bethel carried it too far. That's when he and I had our dust-up, right there in the middle of Mill Street between our two houses. Oh, I was so upset with him, and he knew I was upset."

How could I ever forget their "dust-up?" She *was* upset, no doubt about it. I still shudder at the memory. I watched it all from the front window in our living room. There was my mother compacting herself like a battling banty hen and inching Mr. Bethel back into his front yard. His feet, retreating at a tortoise's pace, finally cushioned onto the grass. Safe on home turf, he raised his hand toward Mom like a safety guard stopping traffic in a school zone. She stopped. He said something, quite a long something, then reached out to shake her hand. She grasped it, leaned in to hug him, and walked slump-shouldered back to our house.

I ducked away from the window and hurried into the kitchen in hopes I hadn't been seen. She entered the kitchen and didn't look at me while she filled a glass from the faucet. She then sat down at the table and motioned for me to join her.

"Mr. Bethel and I have had a discussion about how he is disciplining you. I thought he was wrong, but he is right. I'm the one who's wrong, and I apologized to him. You will do what Mr. Bethel tells you to do. You earned your punishment, and you will take it without complaining."

Mom had closed her eyes. I watched her lying there, a withering subtraction of her former self being kept alive by the oxygen and whatever else they were pumping into her. I wanted to catch a glimpse of the fiery banty hen of yesteryear, but could not. She opened her eyes and rolled her head toward me.

"I was wrong, and I apologized to Mr. Bethel. Do you remember, Rick, do you remember? I apologized to him. What he did was right."

"Yes, Mom, he was right, and I do remember." I held her hand. "Go to sleep. We can talk some more when you wake up."

"Okay, but don't leave. I have something else I want to ask you."

She fell asleep quickly. I settled back in the chair and stretched my legs, but stayed awake.

The Final Visit

I slipped into a high school yesterday,
the one I pass by
on secret walks.
I entered out of curiosity,
wondering if things are
really so different now.

I peeked through
a hallway's windowed door
at a math class within.
The teacher stood
front and center,
while students
in rowed desks
stared at problems
on the chalkboard.

The teacher looked clown-like
with mussed hair and smudges
of chalk dust on his face.
Since no one was smiling,
I guess only I
saw the humor in it.
I caught one student sleeping
and even spied a spitball suspect
cocked and ready.
Everything looked
the same as always.

The bell rang,
and I tried to hurry
back toward the front doors
but was caught
in a swarm of students.
In the crowd
I was—

    bumped and tousled,
    cursed at for being in the way,
    eyewitness to a sneak kiss,
    called grandpa,
    asked for my visitor's pass,
    and told to leave.

Outside and down the sidewalk,
    I turned
        and smiled
            and remembered
and felt happy again.
Humming, I quickened my pace
    back to the nursing home
        before I was missed.

Chapter Eighteen

JIM, A STORAGE CABINET, AND ME

Just before the start of our English class taught by Miss McGee the "Grammar Queen," Jim Cox sauntered by my desk and punched me in the arm. Hey, we were in the ninth grade, and there was nothing wrong with an arm punch. The arm-punching ritual had probably been around for millennia, most likely originating with prehistoric adolescent boys poking one another while scratching out pictographic school assignments on the rock wall of their classroom cave.

Jim Cox, however, had just broken arm-punching's sacred rule and violated its inviolate code of ethics: he had arm-punched me in public.

Arm-punching was supposed to occur in private locations only, like locker rooms or restrooms or parking lots or in the auditorium after the lights dimmed for some program.

Arm-punching was not for public viewing, and it definitely was not to happen in a classroom filled with teenage girls.

To save face, I responded quickly. I jumped out of my seat and punched Jim in the arm, a little too aggressively and a lot too hard. The blow's unexpected force knocked Jim into Tom Hahn's desk. From Miss McGee's front-of-the-room vantage point, she feared she had a mini-brawl on her hands.

Our skirmish was certainly nothing major when compared to school violence today, but it was a legitimate little donnybrook. Miss McGee sorted everything out, and for the first time in my life, I was taken to the superintendent's office. Jim and I walked sheepishly behind Miss McGee as she marched us down the stairs to see Mr. Bethel. We didn't have an official principal, so Mr. Bethel handled all problems big and small. Unfortunately for us, this was about to be defined as big, the awkward situation my father dreaded would someday occur. My brothers and I were students where he was a teacher, and we were repeatedly warned never to embarrass him. Who would have bet I'd be the one to shame Dad and the family? I'm guessing the odds on me were at least ten to one against, with my brother Jeff likely booked at even money.

As soon as we were within the inner sanctum of his office, Mr. Bethel began his lecture. He reminded Jim and me that we were quality young men and role models for the other lads. We should know better than to fight. Our parents expected better from us, and they deserved better. We had not only let ourselves down, we let our classmates down. I remained motionless with my head down and ears ringing. Holy cow! Who'd have thought Jim Cox and I were the school's models of decorum and anointed knights of behavior?

Then came a superintendent's equivalent of a heavyweight champion's punch to the arm. "I am disappointed in both of you."

Crap, I thought to myself, *if Bethel is disappointed in me, what will Dad be? Displeased? Dismayed? Disgusted? Disdained? Disgraced? Disemboweling?* I was dispirited. Mr. Bethel brought my discouraging train of alliterative descriptors to a dramatic halt. He arose from his swivel chair and gestured for us to walk with him.

We dutifully followed him into the outer office where Mrs. Guthrie, his secretary, sat at her desk. *Geez! Could this get any worse?* Marilyn Guthrie, the former Marilyn Angle, was married to teacher, coach, and one lucky man, Charlie Guthrie. After their wedding, most of us guys forgave him for stealing our fantasy. She was the kindest, classiest, curviest secretary in modern history, married or not. She worked in the central office's glassed-in section, an area fully visible from the hallway. Each time I'd pass by the enclosure, I'd wave to her, and she'd wave back.

Mr. Bethel led us to a large metal storage cabinet a short distance from Mrs. Guthrie's desk. He opened the full-length double doors to reveal five overstuffed shelves.

"Mrs. Guthrie and I have wanted to reorganize this cabinet for the past several months but have not found the time. I believe the two of you should use your lunch period to arrange all of these items alphabetically. That is what we discussed, isn't it, Mrs. Guthrie, to have everything shelved alphabetically?"

She nodded.

"Splendid, we are all in agreement. Richard, you and James are to come back at noon tomorrow instead of going to the cafeteria for lunch."

I glanced at Jim, and we gave each other a quick *well, that's not too bad* look. With any luck, we'd be finished before our friends saw us.

We began our task right on schedule the next day at noon, but we didn't have enough time to complete it. Alphabetical shelving is tougher than we'd first thought. We returned the following day and were done with fifteen minutes left for lunch, ample time to eat. Mr. Bethel came out of his office to inspect our work.

"I am impressed, boys, very impressed. The shelves look good, quite good." He patted us on the backs, and Jim and I shook hands to show him we had made peace. "However, you know what? We have changed our minds." He placed a hand on each of our shoulders, not a good sign.

"Mrs. Guthrie and I prefer everything to be organized by size, the smallest items on the top shelf progressing down to the biggest ones on the bottom." He removed a hand from Jim's shoulder to check his watch but kept ahold of me. "Wonderful, you have a few minutes left to begin." He finally let me go.

Jim and I stared at each other for a few seconds before attacking the new task at hand. We made a good start that day, but needed most of our lunch period the next to finish. This time we were even prouder of our results. We stood confidently before the opened cabinet doors and smiled in smugness as Mr. Bethel approached for his inspection. His arms folded, he slowly assessed our work row by row from top to bottom and up again.

"Again, very impressive, very impressive indeed. However, you know something, boys? I think you need to come back Monday." *Oh brother!* "We prefer to have everything organized by color. Yes, by color will make the items easier for us to locate. Don't you agree, Mrs. Guthrie?"

"Yes, Mr. Bethel, I do agree. Much easier."

I could not believe it. Marilyn Guthrie, our one hope for an ally, was in on this, too. My former crush had crushed me. I stared at Jim, and we gave each other an extended *we're really getting the shaft now* look.

Throughout the entire week, our friends had gleefully watched the cabinet rearranging performance from the hallway, mocking us at every opportunity. It was Friday, and now this public humiliation was going to continue into the following week. Desperate, I was down to the only card I had left to play, but it was the trump card and last resort for a weak-willed reformed arm-puncher. I complained to my mother when I got home from school.

Of course, she already knew about our sad saga. Everybody knew. DeGraff had no secrets. Even Auggie Leagre, postmaster for all the years we lived there, heard about it. He no doubt shared my crime and Mr. Bethel's punishment with every entering stamp purchaser.

While I was delivering the afternoon newspapers on Friday, I stopped at the post office to check our mailbox. Auggie greeted me with a broader-than-usual smile. "Rumor is you and the Quincy boy will still be adjusting the superintendent's cabinet next week." He winked. "Tell you what, Rickie, when you finish for the big man, I need your assistance back here." He gestured over his shoulder to a series of multiple-racked shelves holding arriving and departing parcels. "How about you arrange all of them by weight?" He laughed. I didn't.

My complaint to Mom resulted in the infamous "dust-up" with Mr. Bethel. She was upset, and in her mind justifiably so. To be fair, her concern ran deeper than this single incident. It began a few years earlier when I was in the sixth grade, and it involved my archenemy, Elroy Suggs. Elroy entered first grade two years before I did, but he managed to drift back and join me as a sixth grader, his second go-around. He was a classic bully, and for reasons I never understood, I was his favorite target. Elroy was unmerciful verbally and physically, and I avoided him like castor oil.

Through all of our unpleasant encounters, I did manage one brief moment of retaliation. In a dodge ball game during outside recess, I tagged Elroy on the side of his head with a wicked double-underhanded hurl and eliminated him from the game. I didn't have a chance to celebrate. He raced across the dirt-drawn centerline and pummeled me in the face before our teacher, Mrs. Wammes, dragged him away. Nose and lip bloodied, I was sent home for motherly repair.

Then came the open-wound salt rubbing. Mr. Bethel's punishment for Elroy was three days of after-school detention supervised by his gorgeous secretary. How is that for companionship while serving your time? The light sentence infuriated my mother then, and it continued to smolder now into the slow-burn catalyst for her confronting Mr. Bethel in the middle of Mill Street between our two houses. She fiercely argued the point that Elroy's infraction was far greater than Jim's and mine, but he had not been disciplined to the same extent we were. That was her case, that's what she pleaded, and she did all she could to defend it. But Mr. Bethel had effectively diffused her as only he could.

The next evening, she revealed to me what he had said to elicit her apology. She quoted him plainly and directly, and I listened intently to every word.

"Yes, you are correct, Dortha Jean, I am punishing Rick and Jim harder than I did Elroy Suggs. Looking back on it, maybe I should have been more severe with him. But that has nothing to do with Rick and Jim now. Over the years, we have done everything we could for Elroy and have given him as much attention and leeway as possible. We've done our best. But in spite of all we have done for him, he has done nothing in return. I am afraid Elroy Suggs will not amount to very much of anything. Those are harsh words for me to say, I know, and I have never said anything like that about a student before. But what I am saying is true. Rick and Jim will amount to something. You and I both know they will, and they will benefit from this experience. They are learning a valuable lesson. They may not realize it today, but one day they shall. Fair or unfair, that is why I am doing what I am doing. It will make a difference, I promise, and the difference will be as significant as the differences between the two of them and Elroy Suggs."

When Mom finished, she made me promise to take my punishment without any further complaining. And I did. The following Tuesday, Jim and I finally finished the cabinet to Mr. Bethel's satisfaction. Mrs. Guthrie hugged each one of us, and I held on to mine for as long as possible.

Elroy Suggs quit school the following year, still in junior high, bragging he was going to hitchhike to Alaska and join the Forty-Niners in their rush for gold. History and geography obviously topped his list of classroom failures. As far as I know, no one in town heard from Elroy again, and Mr. Bethel's prediction for him was left to be merely an educated guess.

As it turns out, I'd like to think he was correct about Jim and me. Throughout the rest of high school and into life, we did our best to amount to something. I'm hoping Mr. Bethel would have been proud of how we turned out.

Chapter Nineteen ·
OUT OF PLACE

Mom was still asleep when a nurse carried in her lunch. Without either of us speaking a word, the nurse and I agreed it would be best to let her continue sleeping. She placed the tray on the bedside table and asked quietly, "Are you her son?"

Unlike the nurse I'd encountered earlier in the day, this one seemed genuinely concerned. I can tell you from personal experience, family members are appreciative of an understanding bedside manner.

"Yes, ma'am, I am. My wife and I flew in from Arkansas to be with her. My brother thought it was urgent for us to come as soon as possible. We thought this...that Mom might be..." I couldn't finish the sentence.

"I understand," she said, putting her hand on my shoulder. "This is never easy. You were right to come and be with her. Some sons wait too long." She paused a second before adding, "Give me a minute to get her chart. I want to check something. I'll be right back."

Mom stirred slightly but remained asleep. I noticed her fingernails were longer than usual and had not been manicured for some time. She was always proud of her hands, petite and delicate, and routinely kept the nails trimmed and polished with a clear coat. Kurt is the family artist and accomplished metalsmith, and Mom enjoyed showing off his handmade rings. Most of the rings she wore were his gifts to her, but on occasion she flaunted his for-sale items to entice friends into possible purchases. This "human display case" did not mind shilling for her youngest son. Her fingers were now unadorned except for her wedding ring. I was relieved to see that thin band of gold. My mother often bragged she had never removed her wedding ring, not once, during all their years of marriage. After the boast, she also never failed to admonish her husband for removing his once, an unthinkable lack of good judgment that had hurt her deeply.

She and Dad had been playing bridge with their best Oberlin friends, Tommy and Dot Thompson. Between deals, and after a few too many beers with whiskey chasers, Dad and Tommy thought it would be funny to exchange wedding rings, to them a meaningless jest. Before Mom could stop him, the ring was off his finger. In his version of the story, he heard her anguished gasp and replaced it immediately. In her version, his quickness didn't matter. She felt in her heart that an oath had been broken, and his one-and-only time was forever trumped by her never. I continue to be amazed at how life's seemingly insignificant acts can retain lifelong significance.

The nurse returned to the room and motioned me into the hallway. "What's your first name?"

"Rick."

"You know, Rick, your mother has pulmonary fibrosis, correct?"

"Yes."

"Are you also aware she is in the final stage?"

"I figured as much, but what does that mean exactly?" I think I wanted to know.

"Over the years, your mother has received proper medical treatment. And I'm certain your father is an excellent caregiver. But in time the disease overtakes the lungs. When that happens, there is nothing more we can do. No amount of oxygen will help. Her lungs simply cannot get enough oxygen to sustain her."

As she spoke, I looked away from her face and down to her slightly scuffed, white shoes. I wondered if they were comfortable enough for a nurse constantly on the move, room to room and patient to patient. I tried to guess how often she polished them, the number of pairs she wore out annually, and if she had to buy the shoes herself. I wanted to focus on anything but what she was saying.

"Her skin has a slight blue tinge, a sure sign of insufficient oxygen."

I continued to study her shoes. Four eyelets and probably a size seven-and-a-half or eight, but I still heard what she said.

"Yes, I can see that. Her struggle for air is worse today than it was yesterday. We have dreaded this but knew it would happen eventually. I think we tried to convince ourselves it wouldn't."

I finally looked up and into her eyes. This time she looked away.

"I shouldn't say anything else. I really cannot tell you more than that and have probably said too much already." She leafed through Mom's chart. "Your father is meeting with Dr. Sinclair tomorrow morning at ten. I think you should be with him to hear what the doctor says."

"Dr. Sinclair?"

"Yes, have you met him?"

I almost smiled as I replayed the morning announcement: *"Calling Dr. Sinclair. Dr. Sinclair, please report to emergency."*

"No, I haven't. I have heard his name, though. Do you think my brothers can be at the meeting, and my wife?"

"I'm certain they can."

After walking into the room to check on Mom, she stepped back again into the hallway.

"I need to attend to another patient. When your mother wakes up, try to convince her to eat. A little food might make her feel more comfortable."

"Sure," I answered but knew I wouldn't. I'd been down that path before. "Thanks for the information and for your concern. I really appreciate your telling me what you were able to." She gave me a quick hug and headed down the hallway.

I went back into the room and lifted the lid covering Mom's lunch. The small portions included a pie-shaped slice of ham, green beans, applesauce, and a plastic cup of tapioca pudding. The ham's rounded rim was coated with a thin layer of fat. Mom didn't like fat on her meat, so I carefully removed it with the knife. Then I sat. I'm not certain for how long.

Sherée slipped into the room and leaned down to kiss my cheek. Mom continued to sleep.

"How's she doing?" she whispered.

"She's dying," I whispered back.

I walked to the window, its blinds shuttered but leaking narrow slants of light. I pulled the cord and the blinds snapped open. Sunlight flooded the room and splashed over the bed onto my mother's face, waking her.

"Lewis?" She squinted toward the window, and then shaded her eyes before recognizing me.

"Where is your father? I was dreaming I was alone. I couldn't find him." She scanned the room with eyes still adjusting to the light. "Lew, Lew?"

Sherée hurried to her. "Dodie, it's okay, everything is okay. Papa Lewie is downstairs meeting with some people in Admissions. They need more information for your paperwork. Everything is okay. Kurt is with him."

Sherée reached to the nightstand for a glass of water and lifted it to Mom's lips. "Here, take a drink. Everything is okay." Mom sipped at the water and sank back into the bed.

"Dodie, are you hungry? You should try to eat something."

"No, honey, I'm just not hungry. I'll try later."

Daughters-in-law, apparently, can get away with what sons cannot.

"Close the blinds, Rick. That's too bright for me." I returned the room to dimness.

"When is Lew coming back?"

"Soon, Dodie, he'll be back soon, I promise," Sherée assured her.

"I'll take more water. And Rick, please raise the head of my bed a little higher. It helps my breathing." Sherée and I quickly obliged, although the elevated bed seemed to do little to ease her difficulty breathing.

"There's something I want to ask you, Rick, something I've been thinking about. You wrote a poem in college. It was about a flower, a flower without any friends. Do you remember it?"

Of course, I did. At one time, I considered that poem to be my masterpiece. "Sure, Mom, I remember the poem. In fact, I remember it well. I was a student at Ohio State when I wrote it. That was years ago. Why are you asking about it now?"

"I keep a copy of the poem in my dresser. I like the flower, but I never liked your title. You called it *Universal Is Our Love*. Why did you name it that? The poem is nothing about love."

She had a point. "I meant the title to be ironic. I was going through my tragic Holden Caulfield stage, and I wrote it after the girl I was dating broke up with me."

"Poor little Rickie," Sheréc chimed in, "our brokenhearted poet." Mom and I smiled, but Mom's smile lasted longer than mine.

"Okay, Sherée, that was clever. Anyway, during my junior year I entered the poem in a poetry contest. I received an honorable mention, but I was disappointed."

"You should have changed the title. The title was wrong. With a different title you might have won." My mother never ceased to surprise me.

"And, Mom, what would the right title have been?"

"*Out of Place*," she answered without hesitation. "You should have called the poem *Out of Place*. That's what the flower was, she was out of place."

I was puzzled. "Why *Out of Place*? That's an odd title."

She slowly moved her hand to her mouth and paused before answering, "I felt like I was the flower. That flower was me. I understood her. We were both out of place. Sherée, can I have more water?"

I could sense this was an important moment for her, but wasn't certain why. "Mom, how were you and the flower alike? I don't understand."

She glared at me in a way she had not since I was a boy. "No, Rick, no one understood. No one ever understood."

She continued to glare at me, and it made me uncomfortable. I looked to Sherée then back at her. "What is it, Mom? Tell me. I'll try to understand."

Although her constant gasps for oxygen caused her words and sentences to be chopped and jarring, what she'd been holding in for so many years came through to me piercingly and perfectly clear.

"My mother died, and I had to move to Grandma Houchin's farm in Lakeview with my brothers. I was a senior in high school and my father abandoned us. Out of place. I was moved during my senior year, and none of the girls in my class liked me. Out of place. Your father joined the navy, and I went to Lima for a job with the newspaper. Out of place. We moved from DeGraff to Kent. I loved DeGraff and all my friends were in DeGraff. Out of place. We were going to go back to DeGraff after Lew retired, but we went to Arizona instead. Lew wanted to avoid Ohio's cold winters, and I did, too. But again, I was out of place.

And here I am now in this place, out of place. The flower and I, we are out of place. Out of place, and no one understands. Out of place."

This conversation, this admission had left her even more exhausted, and she once again closed her eyes. It had left me wanting to scream, sob, throw something, break something, anything just to let everything out. So much anger, so much grief, too little time. I wasn't ready for this. I wasn't ready. This wasn't fair. None of this was fair.

Mom fell asleep, and Sherée and I continued to sit there holding hands. I felt helpless.

Dad and Kurt eventually returned, and Sherée and I left soon after for Kurt's house. I wanted to shower all of this away. And I needed to sleep.

Out of Place

As a flower, She grew.

> She was a very pretty flower
> with sun-colored petals
> and a sturdy, straight stem.
> "I am beautiful," thought the Flower,
> "just like God promised I would be.
> I am glad I requested to be a flower.
> We have our own world—
> insects, birds, grass,
> trees, soil, and me.
> We will be friends.
> I am glad I requested to be a flower
> and cannot wait until morning
> to meet my new friends.
> Dear God, thank You."

In darkness, the Flower slept.

> The Sun began to rise.
> "Hello, hello," the Flower shouted.
> "Is anyone awake?
> I want to meet
> and learn to know you all."

> *Quiet! Quiet!*
> *Will you be quiet!*
> *Must not talk so loudly!*
> *Too early!*
> *Quiet!*

"I am sorry," said the Flower.
"I am sorry to have disturbed you."
The Flower whispered,
"Must not talk yet.
I will watch and wait."

A spider crept
by the Flower and
eyed a tiny speckled insect
tangled in a web.

"They are friends," the Flower whispered.
"The spider will save him."
The spider killed the insect
and began to eat it.
The Flower gasped but quickly remembered,
"I must not talk, I must not talk,
I will make no friends if I talk."

A bird flew over the Flower
and perched in a tree.
"They are friends," whispered the Flower.
The bird pecked at the tree
and pecked and pecked and
pecked a hole into its side.
The Flower gasped but quickly remembered,
"I must not talk, I must not talk,
I will make no friends if I talk."

A grasshopper leapt by the Flower
and into the grass,
spitting a foul-smelling fluid
onto the blades
and marring the beauty.

It leapt and spit again.
The Flower gasped but quickly remembered,
"I must not talk, I must not talk,
I will make no friends if I talk."

The skies darkened
and rain began to fall.
The comfortable soil
turned to mud.
The Flower gasped.

In time, the Sun shone again.

The insects, birds, grass,
trees, and soil
all sang peacefully
in unison.

But the Flower didn't sing.
She had wilted
and died.

Chapter Twenty
THE GIVERS

It was after five o'clock when Sherée woke me. I couldn't believe I had slept that long and expressed annoyance to her for not waking me sooner. She handled my whining in her usual manner—with indifference.

"Obviously, you were tired and needed the rest. Stop grumbling. I let you sleep and that's that. Now, get ready so we can leave for the hospital."

I know when to listen. I wasn't going to admit it, but she was right to let me sleep. I felt rested and prepared to face the inevitable.

Tucson traffic is maddening almost any time, but it is downright impossible on a late Saturday afternoon. The trip to the hospital took over an hour, and my level of agitation was rising. At one point, I promised Sherée that some day we were going to drive the streets of Tucson at two o'clock in the morning just to experience the thrill of traveling at the actual speed limit.

When we got to the hospital, we found Dad and Kurt in the

room with Mom. Kurt told us Jeff telephoned to explain he was working late and would be there as soon as he could. The lunch tray had been exchanged for a dinner one, and in hopefulness I removed the lid. Nothing had been touched. I recovered the plate and glanced at Kurt. He shook his head and mouthed, "She still has not eaten." By my calculations, she'd not had any solid food for more than two days now. She was existing solely on whatever liquid nourishment the drip bags provided and a few precious sips of water. She looked even more frail and shrunken than she had that morning. But she was awake and talking to Dad.

"What are you two lovebirds chattering about?" I inquired.

Dad answered for them. "Your mother had a dream about Bob. She thinks he was in the room standing beside her bed."

She corrected him. "Lew, it was not a dream, and I do not *think* I saw him. I did see him. Bob was here with me. He was here and just as real as you are."

My Uncle Bob was three when their mother died. After Grandpa Jack abandoned his children, Bob was shuffled household to household until being accepted into a Marsh Foundation facility. Eventually, my parents removed him from the Marsh Foundation's care to live with us in DeGraff.

Although he was an exceptional athlete and decent student, Bob had no desire to attend college after graduating from high school. Instead, he emulated my father by joining the navy. After four years of service, he felt ready for college and enrolled at Wright State University in Dayton to major in history with the goal of teaching and coaching. While in school, he worked as a shift supervisor for a juvenile detention lockdown center in Dayton where he met his wife, Christa. Although she was a youth counselor at the center, she also wanted to teach.

After my uncle graduated, he and Christa moved to Denver in search of teaching positions. Neither found employment in education, and Bob was hired to work as a shift supervisor for a recently constructed juvenile detention facility. The director was pleased to hire a man with Bob's experience dealing with troubled boys. Christa assumed a different type of satisfying position as a full-time mother, raising my cousins Jenny and Jeff.

Bob related strongly to his young wards in the juvenile center, and they to him. Broken homes and early abandonments make for common bonding. He liberally, maybe even literally, poured his heart into his job, so much so that he required heart surgery to unblock his arteries. Since his father had heart problems as well, I suppose Bob's condition may have been hereditary. I don't know for certain, but I honestly think the pressures of his job, combined with all he did for the young detainees, contributed to his need for surgery. The procedure was successful, and he returned to a healthy lifestyle.

My uncle enjoyed following my career and became the only relative I felt comfortable boasting to each time I received a promotion. When I decided to search for a university presidency, we had frequent telephone conversations to discuss the progress. To our shared delight, I was offered two presidencies, one in Iowa and the other in Arkansas. I chose Arkansas, and he was elated for me.

A couple of weeks after my good news, he called to tell me about his bad news. He told me he needed additional heart surgery. He promised to keep me updated, but that was the last time we spoke. Complications set in, and he died soon after the surgery.

The funeral was the same week I'd been scheduled to meet with the University of the Ozarks' Board of Trustees and to be introduced to the campus community. That week, as Sherée and I traveled from Ohio to Colorado to Arkansas, I drifted between sadness and exhilaration and back again, all within a surrealistic swirl of hellos and goodbyes.

Knowing Uncle Bob as I did, I had no doubt he had been in my mother's hospital room. "I believe you, Mom, I believe

Uncle Bob was here. I don't think he ever really left you. How could he? You were there for him when he needed you. Now, he's here for you."

"Thank you, Rick."

Kurt, her truly sensitive son, agreed. "Mom, I believe you, too. He is watching over you like you watched over him." He reached for her hand. "You have always looked out for others and taken care of others. That's your nature, and it began when you were just a girl."

"Yes, Dodie," Dad added. "You are a giver. You have been a giver for as long as I have known you."

I think we were each in our own way trying to explain how much she had given to so many, wanting for her to realize the accomplishments of a life well lived. But words can sound trivial, especially when they are all we have. None of it mattered anyway. She was asleep.

Sherée asked an orderly if there were more chairs, and he brought us two small armchairs from the waiting room. We sat close to one another and away from the bed, waiting and watching. One by one, in respectful tones, we shared remembrances.

Kurt started. "When we moved to Kent from DeGraff, Mom volunteered for Head Start. I looked forward to supper—I think I was only eleven or twelve—because she always had a good story about the kids and some activity she had done with them. She enjoyed selecting a book and leading them in a reading circle. Reading to children was her favorite activity, and she was an excellent reader. She sure had a lot of practice with us and our bedtime stories." Kurt winced and then added, "I also remember the time she announced she wanted to bring a couple of the younger boys home to live with us because she was concerned they were staying in a shelter. Let me tell you, I was afraid I'd be forced to give up my room."

Dad interjected, "Oh, yes, who would forget that? The boys were twins, and for several weeks your mother was serious about it. We had brought Bob into our family, and she was certain we could raise a couple more, but nothing came of it. The twins were eventually taken in by an aunt in Cleveland, I think." He adjusted his chair before continuing. "You know, Bob was like that as well. He'd get attached to a particular boy in trouble and think he could give him the extra care no one else was willing to."

He looked at me. "And, Rick, you are the same way. As a boy, you were a friend to Bernie Jones. He didn't have any friends except for you, and you looked out for him." He rubbed his chin and then said, "I guess I can include myself in this. I was a teacher who tried to do more than teach. Students came to me with their problems, and I listened."

"That's not all, Papa Lewie, don't forget how you have cared for Dodie. I admire you for that." Although Sherée was correct, I don't believe my father considered his taking care of Mom to be anything out of the ordinary. He was simply a man who loved his wife.

"Thank you, Sherée. Maybe looking out for others runs in the family. I hope so. That's a nice legacy, a legacy of being givers."

At that moment Mom moaned, not too loudly but loud enough to concern us. We stopped talking, and Dad hurried over to her. She was still asleep. Satisfied she was all right, he returned to his chair.

I had something to contribute. "Kurt, I don't think I ever told you this, but Dad and Sherée know about it. The first year Mom and Dad stayed in the Ozarks' guesthouse, Mom wanted to volunteer for the Forrester-Davis Development Center in Clarksville. This was a couple of years after she went on oxygen. Forrester-Davis is a place where children and adults with physical and developmental disabilities go to school and work. The complex is a couple blocks from campus. I spoke to the director, but she was concerned about Mom's health and her dependence on oxygen, afraid she couldn't handle the physical demands. Mom was disappointed though, much more so than she let on, I'm certain."

A nurse entered and changed two of the intravenous bags, stirring Mom awake in the process. She asked Mom if she wanted to eat any of her dinner, but she said no and closed her eyes again. The nurse straightened her blanket before leaving with the tray of food. The rest of us retreated to our private thoughts.

I couldn't remember a time when my family had conversed this much without Mom leading us. She was the conversation specialist and our natural guide in topic selection and duration. I tried to imagine how our stories would be different if she were a part of the telling. She was definitely not in conversational shape now with her breathing even more labored than an hour ago. Watching her was painful, and I wondered if she realized the gravity of what was happening. I wondered the same about Dad as I watched him watching her.

She moaned again and weakly tilted her head up and down in slight, unconscious attempts to seize more air. She arched her back, opened her mouth, then settled back, unaware of any of it.

We were all watching her, each of us breathing simultaneously in one collective attempt to gather the room's oxygen and make an impossible transfer. I finally couldn't take it anymore and left in search of a drinking fountain. Sherée rose to join me, but I motioned her away. As I leaned heavily against the hallway's wall, I tried to empty my mind and not think about what was happening. But that was also impossible.

When I returned, Dad had moved to sit in the chair beside my empty one. I sat down, and he asked an out-of-the-blue question. "Cotton and snow, Rick, what's that remind you of?"

"I have no idea. Cotton and snow? I have no idea."

"Come on, of course you remember. Cotton and snow. I know that means something to you. Think."

I was trying but nothing clicked. "Dad, cotton and snow. I don't know what you want me to say. Help me out here."

"Do you remember the cottonwood tree close to our house in DeGraff?"

"Sure, I remember the tree. It was on the old Coonzy property. The cottonwood was behind the house and in the middle of the apple orchard I cleared and mowed for the Bethels after they bought the place."

Dad leaned in toward me. For the first time since Sherée and I arrived from Arkansas, the anxiety had faded from his face and was replaced by the peacefulness good memories can bring.

"When we moved to the house on Mill Street, you were four or five."

"That's about right, I think I was four."

"It was summer, and we did the moving ourselves with Dodie's brothers' help. That day there was a strong breeze, and the big cottonwood was shedding its puffs of white like crazy. Mind you, it was a hot day, at least ninety degrees. Before too long, our front yard was completely covered in white, with barely a trace of grass beneath. We were inside unpacking boxes when you came running into the house. You were yelling at the top of your little lungs, 'Come outside! It's snowing, it's snowing! Come outside, hurry! We can build a snowman!'" He laughed at the thought.

"We stopped what we were doing and ran outside with you. I grabbed up a handful of the stuff and tried to explain to you what it was, that it was just cotton blowing off a tree across the street. You wouldn't believe me, so Dodie and I walked you over to see the cotton coming from the tree's branches. We sat under the tree, the three of us, and marveled at the puffs as they floated their way across to our new home and throughout the neighborhood. Do you remember, Rickie?" He was studying Mom but talking to me. "Now do you remember cotton and snow?"

"I sure do, and you reminded me of something else. The

cottonwood was struck by lightning when I was in high school. Eventually it died, and Mr. Bethel hired Jake Long to cut it down. We counted the rings, and there were over one hundred. Most of the neighbors were glad the tree was gone—it produced quite a mess all along Mill Street—but we weren't glad, were we? We weren't glad because that was the end of summer snowstorms."

The room fell to silence again and stayed that way until Jeff bounded in. When Jeff enters a room, everything comes to life, even Mom. His entrance awakened her, and ignoring the rest of us, he went straight to her.

"How's my favorite girl? Did you miss me?"

"Of course."

He offered an unnecessary apology. "Sorry, gang, but I had to work late. We are trying to complete a major project but keep running into snags. I'm not worried, though, we'll finish on time."

He surveyed the room. "So did I miss anything of interest? Were you talking about me? I'll bet you were talking about me."

Kurt answered him. "Mom saw Uncle Bob. He was here in the room with her."

Jeff's serious side kicked in. "Really, Mom, you saw Uncle Bob? Wow, that is something. Did he speak to you?"

"No, he just stood there smiling. He was standing exactly where you are now."

Jeff quickly stepped back a couple of feet and turned solemn, too solemn for Sherée.

"Well, Jeff," Sheree said. "That's not all we talked about. It seems there was a colossal cottonwood tree close to your house in DeGraff, and Rick thought—"

Jeff stopped her in mid-sentence by raising both hands in the air. "Wait, don't say another word. Let me guess the rest." He cupped both hands to his forehead in a soothsayer pose and spoke in a falsetto voice: "Rick thought when the tree cast off its cotton, like a hairy giant's enormous flakes of dandruff, that DeGraff was having a snowstorm in summer. Am I correct?"

Laughter and light applause awarded his performance, but he wasn't finished. Soaking up the adulation, Jeff raised his hands to his head again. "Wait, wait, I have more. Rick continued to maintain his belief in those snowstorms for every summer until he was a freshman in high school. Then, one fateful day during a general science class, he described the Mill Street Phenomenon—that was his scientific term for it—to his classmates. Mr. Guthrie shattered Rick's fragile snow globe of naiveté with these harsh words of reality: 'That is not snow, dummy. It is cotton from a cottonwood tree.'"

More applause and more laughter. "Am I right, big brother?"

"Ha, ha, good one, Jeff. You have an amazingly twisted memory."

I envied Jeff's gift for telling the perfect story at the perfect time. He cleared the room of morbid thoughts. For the next hour, we shared even more fond memories of a kinder, gentler life in DeGraff. In those precious moments, we forgot why we were in a hospital room gathered around a wife and mother's deathbed.

Nurses entered twice to attend to Mom and to ask basic questions of need and comfort. A third entrance reminded us about the winding down of visitors' hours. Dad insisted he was spending the night, and none of us tried to convince him otherwise, not even Sherée, who he seldom contradicted. We all knew Mom and Dad needed to be with one another.

As we were giving our goodnight hugs, Sherée asked Mom, "Dodie, before we go can we get you something? Does anything sound good to you?"

No one anticipated her answer. "Yes, dear, I would like a toasted cheese sandwich."

A toasted cheese sandwich? Several trays of food had come and gone without Mom taking so much as a nibble, and now she wants a toasted cheese sandwich? We began scrambling around the room and bumping into one another like hapless Keystone Kops in a Mack Sennett movie.

"She wants a toasted cheese sandwich! She needs a toasted cheese sandwich! Where can I get a toasted cheese sandwich?" Rushing up and down the hallway, I was Paul Revere without a horse but on an equally urgent mission. A nurse hurried up to me, and I explained Mom's request. She was calm. "The cafeteria is closed, but someone who can grill a sandwich might still be there. Please go back to your mother and give me a few minutes."

Dad was pacing the room. I think he was convinced that if Mom ate a toasted cheese sandwich, she would be cured, and they could go home to live normally again. I'm certain he believed this was the miracle he had been praying for: the miracle of toasted cheese.

Twenty minutes later, the nurse delivered the sandwich. Dad thanked her and approached the bed with his medicinal plate of hope. Mom motioned him away and said she was not hungry. The miracle melted. Dad collapsed into the chair beside her bed, still gripping the plate and looking as defeated as I had ever seen him. I asked the nurse if we could stay a few minutes longer, and she sweetly agreed.

I sat in the chair opposite Dad on the other side of Mom's bed. Jeff, Kurt, and Sherée stood at the foot of the bed. Mom lifted her head to see us. "I heard a little of what you were saying earlier. Thank you for the kind words." Her eyes fixed on my brothers and me, looking at one of us then another. "But you need to understand something."

She placed her hand to her mouth and kept it there for the longest time, running it back and forth across her parched lips. She gazed at each of her sons again before speaking. "You need to understand this. All I ever wanted in life was to be a good mother and to make everything perfect for my boys."

The things we wish for, want for ourselves and for the ones we love are unique among us. Some wishes are simple, others complex, and many impossible. My mother bound them all.

I answered for us. "Mom, you are a good mother, and we tried to be good sons. But nothing is perfect, except in memory."

That was our last conversation.

Triumvirate

His parents were leading him outside
through the double doors,
father at his side
and mother behind,
arms around
his waist guiding.

The countenance never changed
as they, three unsmiling,
trudged unevenly
down the steps
toward the sidewalk.
His feet shuffled
at a surface
that could well have been
grass or carpet or sand.
Late teens,
maybe older,
he seemed to function
like an infant nursing.

They passed by cautiously.
As his eyes
twisted toward me,
I tried to smile.
Mother looked
to father and to him
and then through me.
I nodded
before turning away.

Later,
as I remembered the scene,
I wanted to cry
but could not.

At Forrester-Davis Development Center
Clarksville, Arkansas

PART IV

Chapter Twenty-One
DR. SINCLAIR

Sunday, December 7th

The relentless ringing of the telephone stubbornly continued, finally waking me up. I squinted at the clock. Its digital 2:18 a.m. face mocked me fully awake. As I've said before, calls past midnight are seldom good news, and this one had little chance of being good. Sherée remained asleep, but I could hear Kurt shouting my name.

I sprang from bed and hurried toward his voice in the kitchen.

"Hold on, Dad, and give me a second to put you on speaker phone," Kurt said. "Rick is here. Start over so he can hear you."

Dad spoke frantically but softly, almost too soft for us to hear. I asked him to speak up.

"I can't talk any louder. I'm using the telephone beside your mother's bed. I don't want to wake her and . . ." in a voice softer yet, "I don't want her to hear what I'm saying." Kurt and I moved in closer to the phone.

"She is having a terrible night, boys, a terrible night. I was going to call sooner but was hopeful she'd improve. I think she's getting worse, and I don't understand why. They gave her a shot to control the pain, but her breathing is more labored. She's been sleeping for the most part. Thank goodness for that. But when she isn't sleeping, she isn't really awake, either. I can't describe how she is. I've never seen her like this."

"Dad, do you need us there?" I asked.

"I don't know, maybe. What time is it?"

"Almost two-thirty."

There were several seconds of silence before we heard him say, "I don't know what to tell you. It's the middle of the night, and I just don't know. What do you think, Rick?" Kurt didn't wait for me to answer. "Dad, I will be there in a few minutes. You stay by Mom and wait for me. We'll get through this. I'm on my way." We told him we loved him.

Kurt grabbed his jacket. "When I get to the hospital, I'll talk to a doctor or nurse, and if this is it, I'll let you know immediately. Jeff can come here and drive you and Sherée to the hospital. If this isn't it, you'll be able to sleep for a few more hours, and then Jeff can pick you up. Remember, our meeting with the doctor is at ten o'clock." Kurt had taken command, and I appreciated him doing so. In those moments I wasn't able to keep focused, but I did notice he was still dressed in the same clothes he had on earlier. Perhaps he'd anticipated this scenario better than I.

"Wait until around seven to call Jeff. He'll probably need to be reminded about the meeting anyway. Now, go back to bed. Doctor's orders." He rushed out.

I decided to call Jeff anyway. He deserved to know what was going on. He answered groggily. I told him about Dad's call and Kurt's willingness to go to the hospital.

"Are you certain it's all right to wait? Maybe I should drive over now for you and Sherée."

I promised him that if Mom's condition worsened, Kurt would let me know, and I'd call him right away. I reminded Jeff about the morning meeting with the doctor and emphasized I'd call him to be certain he was awake. He laughed. "You know me too well, big brother. I promise I'll be over there to pick you up at seven-thirty. Buzz me if anything changes before then."

Although I don't remember sleeping, the rest of the night somehow passed quickly. I nudged Sherée awake a little after six and told her what had transpired. We readied ourselves for what I feared would be a dreadful day.

Jeff was on time. We greeted him in the driveway, but didn't talk much after that as he maneuvered through the surprisingly light Sunday morning traffic. He stopped for coffee and asked us if we wanted anything.

"A miracle for your mother," Sherée answered.

When we got to Mom's room, I walked straight to her bed. Her eyes were only slightly open. She might have been conscious and aware, or she might not have been. I couldn't tell. All of us, I'm certain, felt helpless at that moment. We slowly moved from one to another while making the smallest of small talk. I kept checking my watch, the barely passing seconds extending into barely passing minutes. Thankfully, the doctor came in earlier than our scheduled appointment time.

"Good morning, I am Dr. Sinclair. Is everyone here?" His voice was Midwestern pleasant, and he had a tennis player's tall and slender build with short but styled sandy hair. We all introduced ourselves and shook hands. I sized him up as the direct and deliberate bedside manner type.

"I am guessing you have a number of questions, but let me

give you a brief overview of Dortha Jean's condition first. She has idiopathic pulmonary fibrosis, and in her case, the disease is irreversible. The internal lung tissues are deeply scarred and rigid, and their thickening prohibits her lungs from moving sufficient amounts of oxygen into her bloodstream. Without oxygen, the brain and major organs cannot operate adequately and will eventually shut down. That is what is happening now, and no amount of mechanical ventilation will keep her system functioning." He thumbed through a clipboard. "Mr. Niece, you and your wife have signed a DNR order, am I correct?"

Dad managed to squeak out, "Yes, sir, we have."

"We cannot do anything more for Dortha Jean, but we want her to be comfortable in her remaining time. My nurse contacted one of the local hospice facilities and—"

After the word hospice, Dad harshly interrupted him. "Don't say that! You cannot say that in front of her. She can hear you. I know she can hear you." He moved away from the bed, and Dr. Sinclair did, too.

In a lowered voice he questioned Dad. "Have the two of you not talked about her dying?" He turned to face the rest of us. "As a family, you haven't discussed it?" Our lowered heads answered for us. I looked up to watch his face shift quickly from disbelief to agitation to concern before blending into compassion.

"No, we have not, and I've asked my sons not to talk to her about it either."

I looked at my mother to see if she was showing any reaction—a frown, a twitch, any hint of alarm. Nothing. Nonetheless, I remained cautious. "Dr. Sinclair, is there somewhere private we can continue this?"

We followed Dr. Sinclair down the hallway and into a small room. He closed the door behind him and got straight to the point. "Please listen carefully. Mr. Niece, I'm very sorry, but it's important for you to know that your wife is dying. She may not last the day. Do all of you understand what I am saying?"

178

I was the only one to respond. "Yes."

"We have one concern now and only one," Dr. Sinclair continued. "We want to keep her as comfortable as possible. That is what hospice does well, in fact much better than we are able to do here. My nurse telephoned the director of the Holy Family Center, and she and her staff are prepared to take Dortha Jean immediately. If you agree, I can arrange for an ambulance to drive her there. I will give you a moment to discuss this, but you must decide quickly."

Dad didn't need that moment to consider the situation. "We want what is best for Dodie. You have our approval to take her to hospice. Will I be able to ride in the ambulance with her?"

"Of course you can." He placed his hands on Dad's shoulders. "You stay with Dodie." After Dr. Sinclair moved to open the door, he turned back toward us. "Again, I'm sorry this is happening. Surround her with love. That is the best medicine you can give her now."

After the doctor left, we remained in the room and formed a circle around Dad. He gulped hard before speaking. "Do not say the word hospice in front of her. If she needs to know anything…" Another gulp. "If she needs to know anything, we will tell her she is being transferred to a facility with a more comfortable room."

We all nodded and then made our way back to Mom. The rest remains a blur.

Chapter Twenty-Two
LIFE'S JOURNEY'S END

I followed the ambulance as closely as possible and tried not to tailgate, but I was afraid of losing sight of it in the Tucson traffic. Other vehicles are more polite to an ambulance, allowing it to shift back and forth between lanes, than they are to an ambulance chaser. At traffic lights and stop signs, I could see Dad through the lightly tinted back window of the ambulance. I wondered how he was holding up and if he had yet accepted the certainty of this final journey.

I was driving Dad's damaged Intrepid with Sherée, Jeff, and Kurt as my silent passengers. Well, Jeff and Kurt sat silent. Sherée is the front seat specialist of back-seat driving. I listened to her advice without responding aloud.

"Rick, you are too close."

I'm close on purpose.

"You are driving too slowly."
I am obeying the speed limit.
"You are driving too fast."
Make up your mind.
"Careful, they are about to turn."
I can see the blinking turn signal.
"I should be the one driving."
No argument with that.

I really should have let Sherée drive. Not only is she a better driver than I am, I was distracted, and to be truthful, grateful for her admonitions. She was helping to keep me attentive and all of us safe.

The ambulance turned onto a cactus-lined drive and parked under a protective portico. We had arrived at the Holy Family Center. The two ambulance attendants and a Holy Family employee lifted Mom up and carefully lowered her through the wide back door. When they locked the gurney's legs in place, I realized it was actually a portable bed. I admired the unobtrusive efficiency of medical equipment convenience.

Dad seemed to be in a trance and looked as lost as Mom's description of him when she first saw him standing in front of The Urban Store. He followed the rolling bed through the automated double doors and into the building. We all scrambled out of the car and entered behind them, following them down a brightly lit hallway and around a corner. I'm not sure why, but I checked my watch. The time was 12:25 p.m.

I'd not been inside a hospice facility before and wasn't personally aware of its purpose. In the shortest of hours, however, I converted into their newest disciple.

A lady neatly dressed in white and blue wearing a soft smile approached. I found her expression to be the kindest and gentlest expression I think I have ever seen. Seriously, it was as close to angelic as I am likely to encounter on Earth.

"Are you Dortha Jean's family?"

"Yes, I'm her eldest son," I replied, "and these are my brothers, and this is my wife."

"I am so sorry to bother you, but we need signatures on two forms, then I can take you to your mother."

Years of skepticism have taught me to review official documents carefully before signing. Not this time. With complete trust and faith, I scribbled my name on the papers without reading a word.

While leading us to Mom, she quickly reviewed the hospice mission. "We do everything possible to ensure your mother does not suffer. She will be comfortable and experience no pain. You will be left alone with her, but we are available when you need us."

Simple compassion was their pledge. What more could a dying mother and grieving family ask? When she opened the door and we entered Mom's new world, I could not believe what I saw. The room reminded me of our old living room in DeGraff. Flowered wallpaper, sculpted carpet, an upholstered couch and easy chairs, end tables, decorative lamps, and perfectly placed adornments. Two shaded windows cast the room into tones of muted twilight.

Dad had already stationed himself by Mom's bed, his desperate hands wrapped around her pale fingers. Here, as in the hospital, she'd been placed on oxygen, but I couldn't tell how much of it was reaching her failing lungs. An intravenous probe penetrated her purple-bruised arm. As I brushed by Kurt to examine the translucent bag hanging from the metal stand, he whispered, "Morphine."

Momentarily mesmerized, I followed the plastic IV tubing that began at the bottom of the bag and ended in her needled vein where it fed a constant drip, drip, drip into her grateful body. Nourishment comes in many forms. I raised my eyes to her face, and Mom appeared comfortable and without pain—the hospice pledge.

The others moved in to join Dad and me. I tried to imagine how we looked from the back of the room, circled around the bed in a starkly non-Norman Rockwell family portrait. I reached down to clasp Dad's hand while extending my other hand to Sherée. In turn, we each held the hand next to us with Kurt completing the circuit by taking Mom's left hand. In our many years of familial closeness, we had seldom been this close, banded tightly to keep Mom in and all else out.

A nurse breached our ranks to check Mom's pulse and to sponge slender threads of water along her dried lips and within her mouth. She did not swallow. After a time, the nurse returned to adjust the intravenous drip, freeing more drops to glide faster down the tube. Except for her chest's shallow rising and falling, Mom did not move. The sound of the oxygen equipment was the only thing that filled the stillness of our living room. We breathed as we wished she could breathe, and we waited.

Dad said he was cold, and Kurt was hungry, having missed breakfast and lunch. Promising to return quickly, they left together to get something to eat. Jeff, Sherée, and I remained with Mom.

When it happened, Jeff and I were standing there talking while Sherée rested in a chair. My mother, who had not moved on her own that day nor uttered a word, suddenly shot up from the pillow, her eyes blazing and focused straight ahead toward the foot of the bed. She cried out, "Oh, God, do not do this to me now!" Just as suddenly, she slumped back into the bed.

I couldn't comprehend the moment. Why did she say that? What did she mean? Who was she talking to? I froze, cataleptic in helplessness.

Jeff asked, "Did you hear what Mom said?"

I couldn't answer.

He repeated himself. "Did you hear what Mom said?" He sat down on the couch, his hands covering a sobbing face.

Sherée quickly interpreted a mother's words for her sons. "Dodie is not going to die without Papa Lewie being here. I'll call Kurt and tell him to get your dad back immediately." She grabbed her cell phone and rushed into the hallway.

I stood stiffly, my eyes lasered onto Mom. Her chest continued to rise in the shallowest of breathing. A mantra began echoing through the stiffness of myself.

Hurry back to her.
This must end.

Hurry back to her.
This must end.

Hurry back to her.
This must end.

Hurry back…

Dad and Kurt burst into the room, and we gathered around her. Dad stood to the left of her head, Jeff to the right, Kurt and Sherée each on a side in the middle, and me at her feet grasping both her ankles. I don't know why I held her ankles. It made no sense then and makes no sense now. Maybe I was simply trying to keep her from ascending from us. I don't know.

I watched her chest's slow rising and falling, rising and falling, a vigilant obsession from my childhood. When we lived in DeGraff, from time to time I would watch my family as they slept to be certain they were breathing. I believed if I watched them, they'd keep breathing.

I watched my mother now, a little boy's make-believe that has followed me into the reality of adulthood to this place, to this moment. I watched. Chest rising slower. I watched. Rising slower. I watched. Rising slower. I watched. Stopped. It stopped! I squeezed her ankles tighter. Must not let go, cannot let go. Stopped!

Sherée hurried out to find the nurse. When they returned, the nurse took Mom's pulse, looked at Dad and then at us. She took her pulse again.

What? Tell us! What?

And then the ghastliest, most guttural, plangent gasp I have ever heard and hope never to hear again rattled out of my mother. Chest rises, nurse mumbles, "Slight pulse." Chest rises, rises, stops. Nurse takes pulse, looks to Dad, looks to us, back to Dad. The unearthly gasp I never wanted to hear again, I hear again. Chest rises.

Jeff talks prayerfully. "Let go, Mom, it's okay to let go. Let go, it is okay to let go. Let go." Jeff, the family funny man, the comic among us, the one always good for a good laugh continues to repeat aloud the words we are all thinking. "Let go. It's okay. Let go."

I released Mom's ankles and stopped watching for her breathing. The nurse took her pulse and looked to Dad. In a voice as soft as a church whisper, she affirmed life's journey's end.

I studied my watch. It was 3:40 p.m. on Sunday, December 7th.

We each had prearranged assignments. Mine was to telephone an uncle on each family side and ask him to contact other relatives. I also called Paula Wills and asked her to notify the campus community. There was an irony in my doing this. In past years, reporting responsibilities belonged to Mom. She was always the family clearinghouse for death and all other things serious. I do not want to inherit her job permanently.

I walked outside to a small courtyard behind the hospice facility. The air was chilly, and I shivered while punching in the numbers on my phone: Uncle Richard first, then Uncle Melvin.

My conversation with Uncle Richard was brief and emotional. In his need for closure, he requested details. Mom was the big sister who helped raise him, and he feared she suffered at the end. I assured him she died peacefully, and I know I was most certainly correct. I cannot, however, say the same for us. We suffered. We all suffered. Someone needs to write a manual and title it, *Deathbed Protocol: What to Expect, When and Why*. Maybe I will.

With Uncle Melvin, I was first matter-of-fact, and then emotional. He wanted to know about Dad and made me promise to take care of him. Both uncles expressed sympathy in their own unique and heartfelt manner.

When we left the Holy Family Center, all of us were hungry, and Jeff suggested a nearby Denny's. After the hostess led us to a corner booth and distributed the menus, a perky waitress bounced up to our table. "Welcome to Denny's. How is everyone doing today?"

Dad spoke for us. "Well, my wife of fifty-nine years died an hour ago. She was the mother of these three boys."

A polite waitress pause. "Okay then, you must be hungry. Have you decided what you want?" We couldn't help but laugh.

After giving her our orders, we waited quietly until Dad spoke again. "Can you believe it? Dodie died on December 7th, Pearl Harbor Day. The attack was also on a Sunday. Pearl Harbor was the reason I joined the navy. Can you believe it, December 7th?"

The date continues to live in infamy.

Rick D. Niece, Ph.D.

The Ode My Mother
Should Have Written

CANTO I

I never cry in public,
only within the
privacy of myself.
For then I hear
the silence of myself out loud
and am not bothered
by the psychosomatic
sorrows of others.

Sorrow is less than
a six-letter word
and more than a lifetime.
Some choose to
live sorrow forever,
meandering in circles
in search of
the rainbow's end.
They curse at hands
empty and soiled.

Sorrow waits for me.

CANTO II

Sorrow shadows me,
but out of focus
like telephone poles
blurrily merging together
through a car window
on long back-seat drives.
Sorrow discerns
distant and distorted,
difficult to distinguish
from all else
hidden there,
all the while
knowing
I am here.

Once with Father
I reached toward sorrow
in the wadded-up face
of a half-staff outline crunched
within a bus stop bench.
I was curious to touch
a thing so dead and breathing.
It groaned at me,
and I smelled sorrow
face to space.

Sorrow waits for me.

CANTO III

When I was little,
I sensed sorrow gathering
around my great uncle's
flower-flavored box.
The stark starched dress
Mother made for me scratched,
and I felt odd on Tuesday
in Sunday shoes.
My great uncle
opened one eye
and winked at me.
No one else noticed.
I winked back.

I did not have
a black dress
for Mother's funeral.
I chose my only
dark blue one
and wore school shoes.
I felt comfortable.

Sorrow waits for me.

CANTO IV

Someday
on top of a hill
away from benches, boxes,
and gathering crowds,
I will meet sorrow—
less formal, more permanent—
with my back turned.

Sorrow alone will buckle
my knees with that
grammar school trick,
and I will roll
rolL roLL rOLL
R O L L
in slow motion.

When I awake,
I will rise
turn
curtsy
and cry unashamed
for the whole world
to see.

CANTO V

I am sorry
to introduce
sorrow
to you.

I waited.

PART V

Chapter Twenty-Three
EXIT LINES

We scheduled two memorial services. One was in DeGraff, the other in Tucson at Park West Estates where my parents lived for more years than they had in DeGraff. Dad was a former president of the Park West Association, and Mom served as one of the Welcome Wagon volunteers who greeted new arrivals. They were revered Park West veterans.

A retirement community deals with death on an all too regular basis. The residents plan memorial services and console the bereaved better than most undertaking professionals. The Park West group was remarkable in helping with Mom's service. Sherée assisted George Greenleaf and his wife, Celia, with selecting scripture, music, and the service participants. Several ladies prepared after-service refreshments. I wrote the program notes based upon Dad's recommended theme, "In Memory of a Good Life." Another couple, Al and Marie Smith, printed the programs.

Betty Barnes suggested that Mom's friends give testimonials about their favorite Dortha Jean moments. She prefaced her request by explaining that the "little moments" are the ones we cherish the most and remember the best. During the service, we all learned more about the good life my mother lived.

Leslie and Bob Boll were among my parents' favorite Park West couples. Leslie and Dad shared a talent for music, and Dad often provided the piano accompaniment for her vocal solos during special programs and holiday celebrations. Leslie knew that "Try a Little Tenderness" was Mom and Dad's courtship song, the lyrics perfectly expressing their feelings for one another.

Mom and Dad were engaged when he shipped out during WWII. To be certain his fiancé did not forget him, his voice, or his love for her, Dad made a scratchy phonograph recording of "Try a Little Tenderness." He asked Mom to listen to the song each night before going to sleep. Upon his safe return, he promised to fulfill the lyrics' sentiments for a lifetime.

The memorial service closed with Leslie singing their song. With an angelic voice, she captured their romance, especially as she sang the line about love being their whole happiness.

The "little moments" of life do have meanings of their own. But if we do not pay attention, we risk missing them. They pass by quickly. Sometimes too quickly.

Greenwood Cemetery in DeGraff was once named the most beautiful cemetery in Ohio. At least that was the story told to my generation by the reigning generation, and that is what we repeated to the one following us. The cemetery was a beauty, and no one doubted our statewide recognition.

As a kid, I made many visits to Greenwood to examine the fascinating and mysterious decades-old tombstones. My faithful canine companion Lady, a mixed breed Dalmatian and Greyhound, accompanied me headstone to headstone while I viewed my favorites. As I studied each one, I wondered about who lay beneath. Was the occupant still remembered and appreciated by anyone but me?

Dad and Mom had not purchased our family plots, although I had a special location picked out, but we knew without a doubt that one day we'd be resting among Greenwood's other inhabitants. But life changed, we moved away from DeGraff, and in time none of us lived in Ohio. Being buried in Greenwood Cemetery was no longer practical. I wondered, *would any boys and their dogs visit us?*

My parents, usually the deliberative type, gained sudden spontaneity several years ago and decided to be cremated. They met with the owner of Bring Funeral Home in Tucson and signed a cremation contract. My brothers and I felt burned—okay, that was Jeff's line—because we were not consulted. After our parents' belated but in-depth explanation, we accepted their choice.

They requested to have their ashes scattered on the graves of family members. Mom's family is interred at Walnut Hill Cemetery in New Hampshire, Ohio, and Dad's at Evergreen Cemetery in St. Paris, Ohio. We scheduled Mom's Ohio memorial service for January 7th, one month after her death, with the scattering to occur the following day.

Dad, Sherée, and I drove to Bring Funeral Home to collect Mom's ashes after the Park West service. A dignified Bring associate met us at the front door and led us to a windowless room with mahogany-lined walls, an ornate crystal chandelier, leather-shaded lamps, and plush contemporary chairs. In front of the chairs was an antique-looking pedestal with a streaked marble top. Resting on it was a white container slightly smaller than a shoebox. He did not have to tell us what was in it.

We talked about Mom, and Dad repeated two of his favorite stories. After a few minutes, the associate glanced discreetly at a cornered grandfather clock, and he then delivered our exit line. "Please let us know if we can be of any further service to you."

Now, I know exit lines and consider myself to be expert at them. As a university president, I depend on my exit line expertise and use it regularly to conclude endless meetings, faculty conferences, alumni visits, and unexpected office interruptions. I also adhere to the unwritten rule of exit line etiquette: once an exit line is delivered, the exit needs to occur. Everyone should know that. However, after he issued the exit line, we broke the rule and remained seated while avoiding direct eye contact with him or the box.

Second exit line. "We have been honored to work with you, Mr. Niece, and your family." Again, we did not move.

Third exit line. "I believe you have my business card if you need to contact me." He then sniffed, not a runny-nose sniff, but rather one indicating gentlemanly indignation. It didn't matter. We stayed in our chairs and looked around at everything in the room but him or the box.

There was an additional absurdity in all of this. My mother rarely picked up on my exit lines, in person or on the telephone, no matter how directly I delivered them. And now she was front and center for this exit line fiasco. The bitter truth is that we did not want to leave because that would require one of us picking up Mom's ashes.

Fourth exit line, the implied *you must be idiots if you do not comprehend this one.* "I am late for another appointment."

I wanted to get up, but my legs said no, and I complied. I don't know what Dad and Sherée were using to rationalize their reluctance to move. We sat there in silence for another minute before the associate jumped up from his chair and delivered the all-time world champion of exit lines—he exited. I filed away his move for future use.

Sherée gave me her *this is stupid* look before actually saying the words. "This is stupid," she said, springing up and whisking the white box from atop the pedestal. She walked toward the door, which Dad and I scrambled to open for her. She then led the way to the car and declared, "I am driving. Who is holding Dodie?"

I hesitated, but not as long as Dad, so I took the box from her outstretched hands. It was heavier than I anticipated, much heavier than I thought a box of ashes would be. The significance of the moment seared into me.

I cradled my mother tightly during the drive to Kurt's. When we entered his house, I gently placed the box on the dining room table. No one lifted the lid to look inside until much later that evening.

When we finally did, I was the last to look.

All Fall Down

Ashes
signify
completion.

Flamed to life
in incandescent uniqueness,
ashes burn down
to end up
much the same.

Cigarette ashes
Fireplace ashes
Landfill ashes
Coal ashes
Campfire ashes
Ash Wednesday ashes
Phoenix ashes
(Christianly
honest
mythologically)
are all
after all
simply ashes.

Then
the anomaly,
a category
unto itself—
Crematory Ashes.
Ah, there's the rub
and the contradiction.

Crematory Ashes
last at least
another lifetime,
in temporary permanence,
before evolving
from Ash
to Dust
to Circling
back again.

"Ashes! Ashes!
We all fall down!"

Chapter Twenty-Four
EVERYTHING
EVENS OUT

We celebrated Mom's second memorial service in DeGraff, the small town she always considered home. Since we no longer knew any of the local ministers, having not lived there for almost forty years, Dad asked Fred Houchin, a distant cousin to Mom and father of my boyhood friend Steve, to preside over her service. Though not ordained, his strong faith and spiritual life surpassed most of the seminary-trained ministers I've known. Fred and his wife Connie had remained my parents' lifelong friends, their early bonding a direct result of surviving the shenanigans of their thicker-than-thieves sons.

We invited Steve Schlumbohm to participate in the service as well. He'd outgrown the childish church behavior the two of us had mastered as kids on those Sundays many years ago. Steve is now the most devoutly Christian person I know. Over our years of friendship, I have gained more admiration for him than I can express.

The service was conducted in the Rexer-Riggin-Madden Funeral Home, the Madden being Mike Madden, a former trumpeter in Dad's marching and concert bands. With Mike's detailed attentiveness, Fred's soothing graciousness, and Steve's words of celebration, we were all comforted.

Fred's eulogy was touching, witty, and oh-so-Dode Niece. He struck all the right chords in describing Mom's love for family, education, church, friendship, conversation, and her generous commitment of service to others. He hit a home run as he described her rabid sports fanaticism and joy when watching her boys play. Mom seldom missed any of our games, and Fred accurately pointed out that her referee and umpire taunting voice echoed above the crowd. I must admit her jeers sometimes embarrassed me back then, usually when we were watching Jeff play, and I was sitting beside her. But what I would give now just to hear one more Mom official heckle.

Several others gave testimonies, including my brothers and me. But Uncle Melvin delivered the most meaningful tribute. He reflected on their political debates and heated exchanges, and he confessed they both overreacted at times. He admitted he always learned something during their disputes, a nugget of truth from Mom he hadn't considered, and lamented not complimenting her for her insights.

My uncle's final words brought me to tears. He said that in the end, no matter what their differences were, everything had evened out for him. He prayed they did for her as well. I often think about his message, that in the end everything evens out. I hope he was right and wish I had known his sentiments sooner. I'd have asked Mom about it.

This memorial service also concluded with "Try a Little

Tenderness." Leslie Boll recorded the music in Tucson and sent the cassette to Dad as a gift. The song had gone full circle from Dad to Mom to Dad.

After the service, a meal awaited family and friends at the DeGraff Methodist Church. While the others drove to the church, Sherée and I decided to walk. Remembrances of long ago calmed me as we passed along the familiar streets and sidewalks. Our walk brought us through a section of my old *Bellefontaine Examiner* newspaper delivery route. The houses of Bob and Janet Hall, Andy and Mabel Stayrook, Ernie and Wilda Reeder, Bud and Virginia Amos, and Leota Spain—homes now occupied by new generations of residents—called out to me as their front porches questioned why I'd missed the daily deliveries for far too many decades. I answered by retelling DeGraff stories to Sherée, the only one who knows the repetitive tales almost as well as I do.

As we entered through the massive oak front doors, the inside of the church looked strangely different, even though I had made that same entrance countless times before. Thankfully, the incredible aroma of church-lady-prepared dishes quickly erased any sense of the unfamiliar. The seductive scents led us to their source.

The offerings were laid out on long, cloth-covered folding tables and included shredded chicken sandwiches, sugar-cured ham, candied yams, green bean casseroles, potato salad, coleslaw, deviled eggs, freshly sliced fruits and vegetables, and a special table overflowing with desserts. Jinny Knief's double-custard pie lured me to it, and that's where I began.

The buffet had everything I remembered from past after-funeral meals—everything but my mother's baked beans. I guess these many years later, even among master church lady chefs, no one dared to attempt her *pièce de résistance.* Between savory mouthfuls of delicious food, I accepted condolences. Jinny had set aside a second wedge of custard pie for me, and I ended the meal as I started it.

I have often questioned if funerals actually do provide a sense of solace for the bereaved. As I looked around me at the collection of gathered friends, I vowed to doubt their purpose no longer.

Chapter Twenty-Five
THE SCATTERING

The next morning we went to Walnut Hill Cemetery in New Hampshire. I drove the lead car, followed by Uncle Richard driving Aunt Sally and Cousin Pam. Normally, I didn't like relying on Dad for directions, but this time I hoped the distraction might make the ride easier for him.

Once inside the cemetery gates, Dad guided me down a narrow gravel road to the gravesites. I parked off to the side, and my uncle's car pulled up behind. We crunched our way across frozen grass the short distance to the graves. I had seldom felt so cold, numb from the below-zero wind chill. The piercing winds shivered with us. In life, my mother loathed being cold, and now in her honor, we suffered it for her.

I didn't remember visiting the cemetery before, although I must have. The family headstones were also unfamiliar. With names and dates etched boldly, they seemed to stand out among the others in an attempt to be noticed. Maybe they were too seldom visited and too rarely thought of. I felt bad to be among the neglectors.

Taking charge as patriarch and archivist, Uncle Richard spoke in respectful tones to no one in particular. What he described was obvious, but that didn't matter to us. We were grateful for his narrative.

"Those are my dad's and mom's graves in front, your grandparents. Frank and Elizabeth Houchin, Dode's and my grandparents, are to the right in the row behind them. Grandma Houchin, God bless her, took us in as kids." We huddled closer to hear his freezing words.

"My mother Naomi was the grandmother you never knew. Truth be told, I'm not certain I knew her either. Dode did though, and she kept her memory alive for Bob and me. I was only thirteen when she died, but I still miss her. Isn't that odd?"

He removed a handkerchief from his overcoat's outer pocket and wiped at his face, but the gesture looked to be more of a momentary pause than one born of need. Aunt Sally ran her hand back and forth and up and down his back.

Uncle Richard continued. "This is nice, all of us together. Dode would have liked that. She would have..."

His words, "all of us together," grabbed at me and pulled me back to another time in another place. I went easily.

I was nineteen, and the day was unusually warm for April in Indiana. My tie remained tightly knotted around the buttoned collar of my shirt, but I had shed the suit coat and rolled up my shirtsleeves. Standing within the shadows along the back wall of a funeral parlor in Swayzee, I was looking at my mother and her two brothers through a parallel series of unobtrusive round pillars. Mom and my uncles were stationed at Grandpa Jack's coffin, his propped profile rising above the velvet interior. The tableau they formed was simple yet striking, and for only the second time in my life, I was viewing all of them together as a family. Ignoring raw wounds of the past, death served as an unexpected uniter.

I knew I was wrong to be there, and that I shouldn't be watching this most intimate of moments. I felt like an intruder. I wanted to leave but could not. Uncle Richard, always the most emotional of the three, wept as he leaned down to kiss his father's cheek. My mother and her younger brother waited behind him. When my uncle stepped back, Mom moved forward. She placed her fingers to her mouth and down to her father's lips. With her eyes closed, she held the touch. When she opened her eyes, she motioned for Uncle Bob to come forward. At first he didn't move, and she motioned to him again. He took small, hesitant steps toward the coffin but did not look down. Instead he appeared, at least from my distance, to be staring past the body before him.

He stood stiffly, his face showing no emotion. Then, halt-ingly and in the slowest of slow motions, he stretched out his right hand, palm up, and folded his fingers into a fist. The fist hovered inches above the box. He said something I could not hear. He stopped and spoke again before unfisting his hand. Then falling to his knees, he held onto the coffin. Sister and brother moved quickly to his side and placed their hands on his shoulders while kneeling beside him. The three bowed in unison before their father.

I had seen enough and far more than I had a right to. Embar-rassed by my unpardonable trespassing, I hurried outside to where Cousin Pam was standing on the front porch.

"Where were you? I thought you were coming right out. I've been waiting."

"Sorry." I sat on the porch steps with my head down to tug at my socks. "I thought you said to meet you on the back porch. That's where I've been."

Uncle Richard's voice drew me back to the cemetery's chill. "That's Uncle Ude's stone over there. He is near his sister Naomi and not beside Grandma Houchin. I never understood that. He and Grandma Houchin lived together for so many years, I think they should be closer to one another."

Sherée's warm voice melted through the arctic air. "Papa Lewie, are you ready for this?" She approached him and presented the white box of uncovered ashes.

Kurt crafted unique jewelry, creations that were often his annual holiday and birthday presents to Mom. Now, as a gift to Dad, he had gathered several of Mom's favorite pieces and remolded them into an elegant gold and silver spoon. A portion of its slender handle was forged from her engagement ring. Kurt's spoon of Mom's treasures was to serve as our intimate ladle for her ashes. He handed Dad the token of both grief and celebration.

Somehow not shaking from the cold, Sherée steadily extended the cradle of ashes to Dad. He studied her offering for a moment (or maybe a lifetime) before kissing the spoon and carefully mounding a portion of his love. He scattered ashes over Naomi, over Jack, and then back to Naomi. Sherée brought the box to him again, and he carefully inched his way to the graves of Grandma Houchin and Frank. Standing beside Grandma Houchin's resting place, he thanked her while spreading the ashes of her granddaughter, the motherless child, over the grave.

Dad came to me. "Rick, I think you should be next, then Jeff, Kurt, and Sherée." Seeking approval for his chosen order, he looked to his brother-in-law who simply said, "Of course."

Dad and I embraced as he handed me the spoon. I wanted

to whisper something to him, words of comfort for us both, but could manage nothing before he stepped away to stand between my brothers. Sherée carried the ashes to me, and I filled the spoon.

I walked to Naomi and Grandpa Jack and scattered generously on each. Needing more for Grandma Houchin and Frank, I went back to Sherée. When I finished their graves, I had only a small amount for Uncle Ude, not nearly enough to be respectful. I returned to Sherée for a third time, moved toward Uncle Ude, and knelt beside his grave. I don't know why I knelt since I had not done so for the others.

I spread Mom's ashes from the top of his grave to the bottom, then back to the top until the ladle was empty. I stood and started toward Jeff, but angled instead to Sherée to fill the spoon again. I poured the ashes into my left hand and gave the spoon to Jeff. All else silenced and disappeared from my consciousness.

I hold the ashes. I feel the ashes. I smell the ashes. I examine the ashes. I microscope the ashes to clarity. I try to comprehend them, to recognize them, to reassemble them. Large fragments, small fragments, gritty fragments, jagged fragments, finely dusted fragments. From where was that piece and that piece and that one and that one? I cradle the ashes in both hands, clasping them, squeezing them, compressing them. I grind the ashes, wrest the ashes with all my strength, all my will, all my being. Ashes penetrate my skin, infuse my blood, enter my heart, seek my soul. Find me, find me, find me. I float to Naomi and render to her what remains—from son to mother's mother.

Jeff followed me, then Kurt, Sherée, Uncle Richard, Aunt Sally, and finally Pam. Our tribute complete, we walked back to

211

the cars for the journey to Evergreen Cemetery in St. Paris where the graves of Dad's relatives awaited us and where the ritual would begin again. Sherée volunteered to drive, and I sat in the front seat beside her. Jeff and Kurt consoled Dad in the back.

As Sherée carefully maneuvered the car onto the cemetery's slender road toward the exit, the headstones of my family, their graves renewed with Mother's ashes, reflected in the door's mirror. They were framed and posed for one final look. The mirror's ironic caution, "Objects are closer than they appear," brought the past into focus and beckoned me to the last conversation with Mom.

"All I ever wanted in life was to be a good mother and to make everything perfect for my boys," she had said.

"Mom, you are a good mother, and we tried to be good sons. But nothing is perfect, except in memory."

> *Memories are closer. Memories are closure.*
> *Except in memory, nothing is perfect.*
> *Nothing is perfect, except in memory.*
> *Perfect in memory.*
> *Perfect…*
> *in memory.*

Postscript
BLUE BLUE SKY

After what seems like a lifetime ago, my stories are written, and I give myself a second chance. Sitting in a metal folding chair beside my mother's majestic Queen Anne, I finally read to her. I suspect mothers listen even after death. The cherished final movement of Mahler's "Resurrection" is playing in the background, and all the mothers of heaven listen in as the living room opens wide to a brilliant blue sky.

One mother within the blue, slightly separated from the rest, cradles a baby. While smiling down on the empty chair next to the metal chair where a little boy sits reading aloud, she hums measures of Mahler's heavenly "Resurrection" into the infant's ear. She easily breathes in deep breaths of angel-cleansed air.

And she hears what she already knew.

Her brothers' keeper
Bob, Mom, Richard

Dad's favorite picture

On leave from the navy

At Oberlin College

Life in DeGraff

My high school graduation

Marilyn Angle Guthrie
The superintendent's classy secretary

The man who encouraged me to be an educator

Mothers keep ahold of their children's hands
in spite of passing years and separating miles

Cowboy Rickie

Dortha Jean Geyer Niece

Perfect in memory